THE BATTLE OF CLONTARF

The Battle of Clontarf

Good Friday, 1014

Darren McGettigan

FOUR COURTS PRESS

This book was set in 11.5 on 16 point Adobe Garamond by
Mark Heslington, Scarborough, North Yorkshire for
FOUR COURTS PRESS
7 Malpas Street, Dublin 8, Ireland
www.fourcourtspress.ie
and in North America for
FOUR COURTS PRESS
c/o ISBS, 920 N.E. 58th Avenue, Suite 300, Portland, OR 97213.

A catalogue record for this title
is available from the British Library.

ISBN 978-1-84682-384-8

Printed in Spain
by Castuera, Pamplona

To my niece and nephew
Solas and Daniel

Gáidil for creich ocus Gaill;
It lúatha a n-eich tar Achaill.

The Gael and the Gall are on foray;
Swift are their horses across Achall.

Cináed Ua hArtacáin, *c.*975.

Contents

Acknowledgments

I would like to thank my family, my parents Eamonn and May, my brothers and sisters – Paul (and Cliana and my nephew Daniel), Teresa (and Vince and Tage and my niece Solas), Anna and William (who did some proofreading for me) – and my aunt Ann for their continued love and support of my historical writing. I also want to take this opportunity to thank the many distinguished historians in the then History Department at University College Dublin, who taught me medieval history in my undergraduate days and gave me a life-long love of the subject. These include my first year tutor, Charles Doherty, and later on Howard B. Clarke, Seymour Phillips, Art Cosgrove and Brendan Smith. I think at the time neither I nor most of my fellow students realized how lucky we were to be taught by such a talented group of learned medievalists. I would like to reserve my greatest thanks for my second-year tutor and later supervisor of my MA thesis, Francis John Byrne. It was Prof. Byrne who developed my interest in the Battle of Clontarf by suggesting that, if I really wanted to know about the history of King Brian, the Dál Cais and what happened on the battlefield at Clontarf in 1014, I should read the wonderful articles by Fr John Ryan.

I would also like to express my gratitude to the very helpful staff of the following libraries and institutions who assisted me source and obtain permission to publish the illustrations below: the staff of the National Library of Ireland, especially Dave Phelan of the Department of Prints and Drawings, Berni Metcalfe, Lorraine Peavoy and Honora Faul of the Reprographic Office and Glenn Dunne from the Permissions Office, Aoife McBride and Finbarr Connolly of the Rights and Reproductions Section of the National Museum of Ireland, Síle Coleman of South Dublin Libraries, Sharon Sutton of the Digital Resources and Imaging Services of Trinity College Library Dublin, Maurice Cleary and Mary Conlon of the Office of Public Works, Catriona Doyle of the Irish Museum of Modern Art, Julie Cochrane of the National Martime Museum, Greenwich, Chris Sutherns of British Museum Images, Director Gaylord Dillingham and Luana Lincoln of the Isaacs Art Center, Hawaii, and Gertrud Friedl and Martin Schindler of the Bayerische Staatsbibliothek München. Many thanks are also due to Michael Potterton, Martin Fanning and all the staff at Four Courts Press for guiding this book through publication. Conor Dodd and Adelle Hughes of Whyte's Auctioneers of Molesworth Street, Dublin 2, and the lucky owner of Sitric Silkenbeard's helmet-type silver penny very kindly allowed me to use images of this rare coin. For this I am very grateful. I am also thankful to Tony Sweeney of www.ireland-heraldry.com, and Anne Christina Sørenson and Rikke Johansen of the Viking Ship Museum, Denmark, for their help in sourcing illustrations.

Finally, I would like to thank the following people: my friends Emmett and Emer O'Byrne, Joe and Estefania McNabb, Ronan and Caroline LeLu, Paul and Gillian McGuill and Tony and Emily McCormack (and all the children of the above), Terry Clavin, Gavin Slattery, Emma Rice and Sinéad McNabb, all my Wicklow, Rathnew and Donegal relations, especially my aunt and uncle Frank and Marion McGettigan, my aunt Josephine Walsh in New Zealand, my granduncle and grandaunt John and Bridget McGettigan, my grandaunt Kathleen McGettigan (who took some photographs for this book) and my cousins Frank McGettigan and Caroline O'Sullivan. I also want to thank Tadhg Ó hAnnracháin, Colonel Donal O'Carroll, my former colleagues in the FCA, Joe Jacob, Jack Ryan, Caroline Brown and Denis Teevan, my secondary school teachers, my undergraduate classmates and my later tutorial students and the many other people in Co. Donegal who have supported my research over the years. I would like to assure these people that I hold them in the very highest regard.

Dublin, Easter 2013

Abbreviations

AFM	*Annals of the Four Masters*, ed. John O'Donovan (Dublin, 1856)
AI	*The Annals of Innisfallen*, ed. Seán Mac Airt (Dublin, 1988)
ALC	*The Annals of Loch Cé: a chronicle of Irish affairs from AD1014 to AD1590*, ed. William Hennessy (London, 1871)
ASC	*The Anglo-Saxon Chronicles*, ed. Michael Swanton (London, 2003)
AT	*The Annals of Tigernach*, ed. Whitley Stokes (reprinted from *Revue Celtique* 1896/7, Felinfach, 1993)
AU	*The Annals of Ulster (to AD1131)*, ed. Seán Mac Airt and Gearóid Mac Niocaill (Dublin, 1983)
BM	British Museum
CGRG	*Cogadh Gaedhel re Gallaibh: War of the Gaedhil with the Gaill*, ed. James Henthorn Todd (London, 1867)
CS	*Chronicon Scotorum: a chronicle of Irish affairs from the earliest times to AD1135: with a supplement containing the events from 1141 to 1150*, ed. William Hennessy (London, 1866)
DIB	*Dictionary of Irish biography*, ed. James McGuire and James Quinn (Dublin, 2009)
IHS	*Irish Historical Studies*
IMMA	Irish Museum of Modern Art
JCHAS	*Journal of the Cork Historical and Archaeological Society*
JRSAI	*Journal of the Royal Society of Antiquaries of Ireland*
NLI	National Library of Ireland
NMM	National Maritime Museum, Greenwich
OPW	Office of Public Works
PRIA	*Proceedings of the Royal Irish Academy*
TCD	Trinity College Dublin

Introduction

On the morning of Good Friday, 23 April 1014, two large armies faced off against each other in the fertile and wooded area of Clontarf (in Irish *Cluain Tairbh* 'the plain, lawn, or meadow of the bulls'), north of the River Liffey and the town of Dublin, by the shore of Dublin Bay. The more numerous force, comprising Munster warriors with a contingent from south Connacht, was commanded by Murchad, the capable favoured son of the high-king of Ireland, Brian Boru. If the later sagas are to be believed (which, in this respect, they are likely to be), Brian himself was present behind the Munster battle-line, praying for victory, surrounded by a bodyguard formed up into a small shieldburg. Opposing the high-king's army was a smaller but much more heavily armed and armoured force made up of Scandinavian warriors from the islands to the north and west of Scotland, the Isle of Man and the town of Dublin, along with a small army of Leinstermen, commanded by Sigurd Hlodvisson the Stout, jarl (Old Norse for earl, a deputy to a king) of Orkney, and Máelmórda king of Leinster. The Scandinavians were well armed with sword and axe, and were clad in metal helmets and shirts of mail. Although medieval Irish warriors are sometimes depicted in bardic poetry as wearing 'shirts of thin satin' into battle, these descriptions may be stylized and inaccurate. The Munstermen were most likely wearing some form of leather armour and helmet at Clontarf. They were still at a definite disadvantage, however, during the ensuing encounter against the 'foreigners of the armour'.[1]

As the later Icelandic Njal's Saga put it, 'the ranks went at each other. The fighting was very fierce'.[2] Indeed, the battle lasted nearly all day and most of the major figures on both sides were killed. The Munster warriors appear to have gained the upper hand as the fighting progressed, owing to superior numbers and also to massive volleys of spears, which were the Irish

1 Nicholas Williams (ed.), *The poems of Giolla Brighde Mac Con Midhe* (Dublin, 1980), pp 140–1; *CGRG*, pp 202–3. 2 Robert Cook (ed.), *Njal's Saga* (London, 1997), pp 301–3.

weapon of choice in 1014. Njal's Saga recounts that Jarl Sigurd of Orkney was killed by an Irish spear.[3] Murchad, the high-king's son, also fell in the battle (he may have died of his wounds the next morning). Many more of Brian's close family and most important adherents were also killed. In the end, the Vikings and Leinstermen ran and were massacred all the way to the gates of Dublin, handing the high-king and his army a tremendous victory. Tragedy ensued. Abandoned by most of his bodyguards, who had joined in the pursuit, and almost alone, Brian was attacked and killed by Brodir, the commander of the warriors from the Isle of Man.

These events became famous all over Ireland and the Scandinavian world. The battle was commemorated in many sagas, both Irish and Icelandic, and in Irish folklore for centuries to come. This short book is my attempt, as an early modern historian who has had an interest in the Battle of Clontarf for many years, to write an accurate narrative of the events of that April day almost one thousand years ago. Chapter 1 puts the Battle of Clontarf within the context of the history of the island and the earlier Viking invasions. Beginning with the momentous events of the early tenth century, this chapter focuses on the invasion of Ireland by the Viking raiding dynasty, the grandsons of Ívarr. This highly capable group re-founded Dublin and defeated the Uí Néill high-king at the Battle of Dublin in 919. The grandsons of Ívarr, however, neglected the conquest of the Irish interior for a more lucrative seizure of the city of York. As a result, they left themselves vulnerable to future subjugation by the Anglo-Saxon kings of England. These themes are all examined in this chapter. Also discussed is the extent of Scandinavian settlement in Dublin and southern Ireland, intermarriage between the Scandinavian and Irish royal families and some important aspects of Irish culture in the tenth century such as Christianity on the island, the Irish warrior tradition and the high-kingship. The Cenél nEógain dynasty is used as an example, given their great success against the Viking invaders of the north of Ireland.

Chapter 2 charts the rise of Brian's family and his eventual seizure of the

3 Ibid., p. 302.

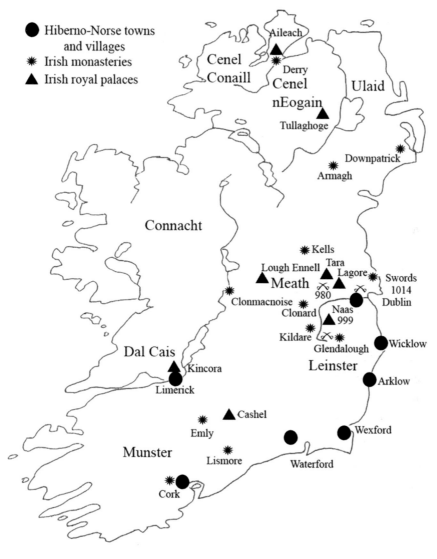

● Hiberno-Norse towns
   and villages
✳ Irish monasteries
▲ Irish royal palaces

Aileach ▲

Cenel
Conaill

Derry ✳
Cenel
nEogain

Ulaid

▲
Tullaghoge

✳ Downpatrick
✳
Armagh

Connacht

✳ Kells

Tara
Lough Ennell ▲ Lagore ✳ Swords
▲ Meath   ▲ 1014
✳   980   ● Dublin
Clonmacnoise ✳
Clonard ✳   Naas
  ▲ 999
✳
Kildare   ● Wicklow
  Glendalough
Leinster   ● Arklow

Dal Cais

▲ Kincora
●
Limerick

▲ Cashel

✳ ● Wexford
Emly
Munster   ✳
  Lismore   ● Waterford

✳ ●
Cork

1 Map of the island of Ireland, AD1000.

high-kingship from the Uí Néill. The narrative here departs from the traditional story that has until now appeared in most accounts of Brian Boru.
My focus is on the Uí Néill high-kings and when they first took serious
notice of Brian. This chapter discusses what is known about Brian's dynasty,
the Dál Cais, and his route to power, which is not a great deal. The analysis

2 Map of Atlantic Europe, AD1000.

is confined to primary sources to avoid the speculative and sometimes quite unreliable accounts of Brian's early life and the history of the Dál Cais that have appeared in print elsewhere. The remainder of this chapter follows Brian through his conquest of all Ireland, focusing on his subjugation of the powerful Uí Néill kings. The first to submit was Máelsechnaill II, a highly respected and successful king of Meath. Brian had great difficulty in conquering Flaithbertach Ua Néill, the king of Cenél nEógain, the final powerful independent king on the island. His successful cultivation of a good relationship with the great monastery of Armagh facilitated this. The manner in which this helped to consolidate Brian's island-wide authority is also analysed.

Chapter 3 looks at the Anglo-Saxon and Scandinavian backgrounds to the Battle of Clontarf, very little of which has been addressed in detail before. These were important arenas that contributed to events in Ireland around the year 1014. My analysis begins with the commencement of the second great Viking attack on Anglo-Saxon England, led by Scandinavian leaders such as the Norwegian Olaf Tryggvason. Olaf had close associations with Ireland earlier in his life. By the beginning of 1014, these Vikings, now under the command of Svein Forkbeard of Denmark, had conquered the entire Anglo-Saxon kingdom. This must have affected Ireland by unsettling the powerful Hiberno-Norse king of Dublin, Sitric Silkenbeard. Sitric almost certainly decided to throw off Brian's overlordship in 1013 and exchange it for that of Svein of Denmark. In this chapter, I also explore the history of the jarldom of Orkney and the career of Jarl Sigurd Hlodvisson the Stout, who was to fight at Clontarf. Areas covered include what is known about the Scandinavian settlement of the Scottish islands before the early eleventh century, as well as the growth in power of Sigurd's strength in the north of Scotland and the Hebrides in the decades before 1014. There is also some discussion of Scandinavians from the Isle of Man.

Chapter 4 narrates the lead up to and actual course of events during the Battle of Clontarf. Only events for which evidence exists are included. These begin with the rebellion in the year 1012 of King Flaithbertach Ua Néill of Cenél nEógain, which Brian initially failed to adequately suppress. It was this failure that led Sitric Silkenbeard, assisted by his ally the king of Leinster, to rebel in 1013. The importance of the death of Svein Forkbeard in early 1014 (he died unexpectedly in his sleep) is also discussed, as this had the potential to leave the king of Dublin isolated. Sitric was undaunted by this setback, however, and recruited Jarl Sigurd Hlodvisson of Orkney and Brodir of Man to fight for him later in 1014. This chapter also details Brian's campaign in 1013, a campaign in which his son Murchad took a prominent part. This is followed by Brian's gathering of his forces in 1014 (the Munster army and a contingent from south Connacht). My account of the battle follows. I show how the various sagas are unreliable but that it is possible to recreate some aspects of the battle using other more reliable primary source material. The book suggests that Murchad's role on the day of battle was important. The size and layout of the opposing armies are carefully estimated, as is what may have occurred during the fighting. An important piece follows, dealing with the death of Brian and the end of the battle. An analysis of the immediate aftermath and events up to the 1040s and 1060s ends the narrative. In the conclusion, the importance of the Battle of Clontarf is assessed. Comparisons with other influential medieval battles on these islands, such as Hastings (1066) and Bannockburn (1314), are made. The impact of the battle on the subsequent history of the Dál Cais, the jarldom of Orkney, the Uí Néill high-kingship and the Hiberno-Norse town of Dublin are also discussed.

THE HISTORICAL AND SAGA SOURCES FOR THE BATTLE

There are entries on the battle in most of the major Irish annals, and Irish and Scandinavian saga material relating to the conflict at Clontarf is rich in both traditions. The Irish annals are medieval and early modern chronicles, divided into yearly segments, which record the most important or unusual events that occurred each year. These are usually battles and obituaries of prominent people. Icelandic sagas are more a combination of 'authentic history, the inventions of oral tradition, written sources and the contributions of the thirteenth-century author'.[4] Unfortunately, sagas are not what would today be regarded as accurate or satisfactory primary source material. The most reliable record of the battle is preserved in the Annals of Inisfallen, 'the oldest major collection of annals which have survived'.[5] This is a Munster compilation and around the time of the Battle of Clontarf it appears to have been recorded at the great monastery at Emly. Brian's brother Marcán was coarb (*comharba* is an Irish medieval term for an abbot who succeeded to the authority and revenues of the founder of an early monastery) there from 990 until his death in 1010.[6] Another reliable annalistic account should have come from the Annals of Ulster. Generally

4 Ibid., pp xiii–xiv. 5 Timothy O'Neill, *The Irish hand* (Portlaoise, 1984), pp 20–1.
6 *AI*, 990, 1010, 1014; definition is taken from Katharine Simms, *From kings to warlords* (Bury St Edmunds, 1987), p. 173.

regarded as 'the most trustworthy of all the Irish annals', AU were compiled
by Cathal Óg MacMaghnusa, a learned cleric from Fermanagh who died in
1498.[7] The entry for the Battle of Clontarf in 1014 in these annals appears
to have been corrupted somehow, in relation to a number of names
recorded as casualties and especially in its reference to a force of '1,000
Scandinavian breastplates'.[8] The influence over the years of Irish saga
material relating to the battle may be responsible for this.

The Annals of the Four Masters, an early seventeenth-century compilation, also has an informative account of the Battle of Clontarf. This set of
annals continues many of the inaccuracies of earlier annalistic records,
however, as well as introducing a prominent pro-King Máelsechnaill II of
Meath bias that is pure Uí Néill propaganda.[9] There is another group of
Irish annals associated with the monastery of Clonmacnoise that have this
same bias. These are the Annals of Tigernach, which range from early Irish
legendary history up to the year AD1088, with a number of gaps.[10]
Unfortunately for the study of the Battle of Clontarf, the years 1002 to 1017
are missing from these annals.[11] Two other sets of annals with this same pro-
Uí Néill bias were written in the seventeenth century but are based on
much older original compilations. These are the Chronicon Scotorum,
written by Dubhaltach Óg Mac Firbhisigh before 1650 and the Annals of
Clonmacnoise, translated into English from an 'ould Irish book' by Conall
Mageoghegan in 1627.[12] Another late set of annals, the Annals of Loch Cé,
that were written towards the end of the sixteenth century and cover the
years 1014 to 1590, actually begin with an extensive account of the Battle of

7 O'Neill, *The Irish hand*, pp 50–1.   **8** *AU*, 1014; Máire Ní Mhaonaigh, *Brian Boru:
Ireland's greatest king?* (Stroud, 2007), pp 54–7.   **9** *AFM*, 1013 [*recte* 1014].
10 O'Neill, *The Irish hand*, pp 28–9.   **11** *The Annals of Tigernach*, vols 1 and 2, repr.
from *Revue Celtique* 1895/6 and 1896/7 (Felinfach, 1993).   **12** William Hennessy (ed.),
*Chronicom Scotorum: a chronicle of Irish affairs, from the earliest times to AD1135; with a
supplement containing the events from 1141 to 1150* (London, 1866); Vincent Morley,
'Dubhaltach Óg Mac Firbhisigh', James McGuire and James Quinn (eds), *Dictionary of
Irish biography*, 5 (Cambridge, 2009), p. 1008; Denis Murphy (ed.), *The Annals of
Clonmacnoise, being Annals of Ireland from the earliest period to AD1408, translated into
English AD1627 by Conell Mageoghan* (Dublin, 1896); Darren McGettigan, 'Conall
Mageoghegan (Mac Eochagáin)', *DIB*, 6, pp 250–1.

Clontarf. This set of annals is missing its first pages.[13] Although the account of the battle given in this source is interesting and introduces some new facts not found anywhere else, it has obviously been greatly influenced by saga material. As a result, the entry for the year 1014 is too corrupt to be relied upon for any unique information. For example, these annals state that Brian's nephew, Conaing, was praying alongside him behind the shield wall at Clontarf where he was also killed.[14]

The surviving saga material relating to the Battle of Clontarf is very rich. This includes Icelandic sagas that mention the Battle of Clontarf in passing while dealing mainly with other subjects and the major Irish saga of King Brian's career and the Viking Wars, *Cogadh Gaedhel re Gallaibh* (*CGRG*) (War of the Irish with the Foreigners). These accounts are legendary and full of fantasy and folklore. They may contain accurate pieces of information but it is impossible now to know which are legendary and what is factual. *CGRG* is dynastic propaganda commissioned by King Brian's descendants that dates from the early twelfth century.[15] It is associated with Brian's most successful descendant, his great-grandson, Muirchertach Ua Briain, who died in 1119.[16] The saga is graphic and remarkable but clearly a legendary account of the Viking wars in Ireland. The saga devotes a large amount of space to the legends associated with Brian's early life and his subsequent career as high-king that ultimately led to the Battle of Clontarf. *CGRG* also contains a vivid and extended description of the battle, very little of which is useful for reconstructing the events of 1014. While *CGRG* does have a generally chronologically accurate framework, it is full of references to people, speeches and an account of the Battle of Clontarf that are clearly legendary.[17] Nevertheless, it is highly entertaining propaganda and must have greatly assisted the career of Brian's great-grandson.

The Icelandic sagas do not deal directly with the Battle of Clontarf but contain accounts of it of varying extent. The longest description is in Njal's

---

13 *ALC*, p. xxxi and the entry for 1014. **14** Ibid., 1014. **15** James Henthorn Todd (ed.), *Cogadh Gaedhel re Gallaibh: War of the Gaedhil with the Gaill* (London, 1867). **16** *AU*, 1119; *AI*, 1119. **17** Máire Ní Mhaonaigh, 'Cogad Gáedel re Gallaib and the annals: a comparison', *Ériu*, 48 (1996), 101–26.

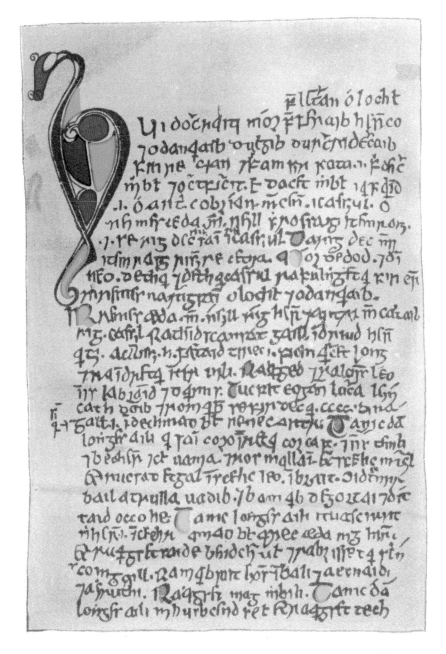

3 The opening passage of *Cogadh Gaedhel re Gallaibh* (*CGRG*), from the twelfth-century Book of Leinster. This cleaned image of how the folio may originally have appeared was created by James Henthorn Todd, the nineteenth-century editor of *CGRG*; taken from Henthorn Todd, *CGRG* (London, 1867).

Saga, a highly regarded family saga. Njal's Saga is primarily concerned with feuding in Iceland in the late tenth and early eleventh centuries. In particular, Njal's Saga deals with the burning to death of a man called Njal Thorgeirsson in his house at Bergthorshvol in southern Iceland in the year 1010.[18] The saga has a strong Christian element to it (Iceland converted to Christianity in AD1000), and it deals with the Battle of Clontarf when a number of Icelanders have to leave their homeland and take service with Sigurd Hlodvisson the Stout, jarl of Orkney. Sigurd brings the Icelanders with him in the force he takes to Dublin, where they are nearly all killed at Clontarf. Many legends and strange portents before and after the battle are recounted and Brian appears as a saintly figure in this saga. It is believed that Njal's Saga was written in Iceland about the year 1280.[19] Orkneyinga Saga is a saga history of the jarls of Orkney from the ninth to the thirteenth centuries. It has a paragraph on the Battle of Clontarf. This deals with the death of Jarl Sigurd Hlodvisson in the battle.[20] This saga was compiled about the year 1200 by an Icelander with Orkney connections.[21] These are the main Scandinavian sources for the Battle of Clontarf.

An Irish monk called Marianus Scottus, who lived in Germany from the time of his exile from Ireland in 1056 to his death in 1082, wrote a 'world chronicle' called *Chronicon ex chronicis*. This source contains a very significant reference to the Battle of Clontarf that has an important bearing on the saga material just mentioned. The Chronicon has an entry for 1014 that states that Brian Boru 'was slain while at prayer' in the lead up to Easter, thus indicating that the account of Brian's death given in the later Irish and Scandinavian sagas was already well known by 1072, by which time much of the Chronicon had been written.[22] A Frankish chronicler, Ademar of Chabannes, a learned monk who was born c.989 in the Limoges region of France and who died on pilgrimage to Jerusalem in 1034, also made a near

---

18 *Njal's Saga*, p. viii. **19** Ibid., pp ix, xiii. **20** Hermann Pálsson and Paul Edwards (eds), *Orkneyinga Saga: the history of the earls of Orkney* (St Ives, 1978), p. 38. **21** Ibid., p. 9. **22** Bartholomew MacCarthy (ed. and trans.), *The Codex Palatino-Vaticanus, 830* (Dublin, 1892), pp 4–15; Benjamin Hudson, 'Marianus Scottus' in Seán Duffy (ed.), *Medieval Ireland: an encyclopedia* (New York, 2005), p. 320; Aidan Breen, 'Marianus Scottus (Máel Brigte)', *DIB*, 6, pp 359–60; Ní Mhaonaigh, *Brian Boru*, pp 57–9.

contemporary record of the events at Clontarf in his own *Chronicon*.[23] Ademar as a chronicler was interested in the warfare between the Christian peoples situated on the western periphery of Europe and various pagan invaders such as the Scandinavians and the Muslim Saracens. As a result, his *Chronicon* has information on Anglo-Saxon England and northern Spain for this period. That Ademar also took notice of the Battle of Clontarf, one of the most prominent events to take place in Atlantic Europe in the year 1014, is therefore not surprising. The medieval Welsh source known as *Brut Y Tywysogyon* or 'The Chronicle of the Princes' also records a good account of the Battle of Clontarf, which comprises its entire entry for the year 1014. Owing to the proximity of the Isle of Man to north Wales, the Chronicle of the Princes gives a prominent role in the events surrounding the great battle to Brodir of Man.[24]

The folk-memory of the Battle of Clontarf was kept alive by the Gaelic Irish population of the island for centuries after the events of 1014. The nineteenth-century Irish historian John O'Donovan, who took a great interest in the history surrounding the battle, discovered some folklore among the O'Kellys of Connacht in the early 1800s concerning their ancestor Tadhg Ua Ceallaigh, the king of Uí Máine, who was killed in the great battle. In 1856, O'Donovan wrote:

> according to a wild tradition among the O'Kellys of this race, after the fall of their ancestor, Teige Mor, in the Battle of Clontarf, a certain animal like a dog (ever since used in the crest of the O'Kellys of Hy-Many), issued from the sea to protect his body from the Danes, and remained guarding it till it was carried away by the Ui-Maine.[25]

---

23 P. Bourgain (ed.), 'Ademari Cabannensis Chronicon', *Corpus Christianorum: Continuatio Mediaeualis*, 129 (Turnhout, 1999), pp vii–xiii. **24** Thomas Jones (ed.), *Brut Y Tywysogyon or The Chronicle of the Princes, Peniarth MS 20 Version* (Cardiff, 1952/85), 1014, p. 11. **25** *AFM*, 1013 [*recte* 1014] (note m).

4 The late medieval coat of arms of the O'Kellys of Uí Máine showing the green dog-like creature that forms the crest. According to a legend preserved in the family for centuries, this strange animal emerged from the sea at the Clontarf battlefield in 1014 to protect the dead body of King Tadhg Ua Ceallaigh until it was recovered by his followers (courtesy of www.-ireland-heraldry.com).

This is a remarkable piece of early collected folklore. O'Donovan also recorded that 'according to the tradition in the country, the Connachtmen were dreadfully slaughtered in this battle, and very few of the O'Kellys, or O'Heynes, survived it'.[26]

26 Ibid.

1 Ireland and the early Viking invasions

In medieval times, the appearance of a comet was often taken as a bad omen, and the tenth and eleventh centuries were an active period in the sky above Ireland. In a dramatic entry for the year 917, AU record 'horrible portents also: the heavens seemed to glow with comets; and a mass of fire appeared with thunder in the west beyond Ireland, and it went eastwards over the sea'.[1] In 912, the same annals record that a comet appeared, while in 911 they record that 'two suns ran together on the same day' (6 May).[2] Events such as these (the record of 917 appears to have been the passage of a large meteor over Ireland) no doubt frightened the mass of the population who did not understand such natural phenomena and who attributed sinister supernatural meaning to them.[3] Indeed, great misfortune befell Ireland in the year 914 when a Viking raiding dynasty known as the grandsons of Ívarr (the Ua Ímair) descended on the coast, seizing and fortifying Waterford in 914 and Dublin in 917, and raiding into the interior of Ireland to such an extent that it appeared that the entire island was about to be conquered by the Vikings. Viking raiders, initially mostly from Norway, had been raiding the coasts and up the rivers of Ireland since around the year 800. The ninth century saw these raids intensify with the first building of ship forts (*longphuirt*) and then a number of permanent Scandinavian settlements on the coast, usually at strategic points on the borders between Irish kingdoms. These periods of raiding were often interspersed with times of peace, and the first Vikings were expelled from the island in 902. In 914, the Vikings returned. The grandsons of Ívarr were descended from Ívarr the Boneless, a leader who was active in the conquest of the Anglo-Saxon kingdoms of East Anglia and Northumbria in the 860s, whom AU called upon his death in 873 'king of the Norsemen of all Ireland and Britain'.[4] In

---

1 *AU*, 917.   2 Ibid., 912, 911.   3 For example, see the reaction of the Anglo-Saxons of England to the appearance of Halley's Comet in the sky over their kingdom in 1066, Michael Swanton (ed.), *The Anglo-Saxon Chronicles* (London, 1996), 1066; David Wilson, *The Bayeux Tapestry* (London, 1985), p. 182.   4 *AU*, 873; Howard Clarke,

914, they were led by his grandsons Sitric, Ragnall and Gofraid, the last of whom was called by the Irish 'a most cruel king of the Norsemen'.[5]

The grandsons of Ívarr refounded Dublin (*Dyflinn*) in 917 on a slight ridge overlooking the River Liffey above the *linn duib* (the black pool), a tidal pool on the River Poddle where it flowed into the Liffey.[6] The grandsons of Ívarr also refounded the town of Waterford (*Veðrarfjorðr*, the windy fjord). In 917, Sitric Ua Ímair defeated the Leinstermen at the Battle of Ceann Fuait, fought at a *longphort* near Leixlip on the Liffey. The grandsons of Ívarr killed the king of Leinster and many of his sub-kings and nobles.[7] In 919, the grandsons of Ívarr killed the high-king of Ireland, Niall Glúndub, at the Battle of Dublin.[8] It was at this point that the island of Ireland appeared to be about to fall to the Vikings. In the years after the Battle of Dublin, the grandsons of Ívarr plundered many wealthy monasteries such as Kells and Armagh and fleets were sent north to harass the Northern Uí Néill dynasties of Cenél Conaill and Cenél nEógain.[9] The grandsons of Ívarr then decided to focus on gaining control of the wealthy city of York in Scandinavian Northumbria in northern England. This drew the Viking warriors away from a conquest of the Irish interior, across the Irish Sea to England and Scotland. Ragnall Ua Ímair appears to have won control of York in 918. When he died in 921 he was succeeded by his brother Sitric, who in turn was succeeded by Gofraid Ua Ímair. Gofraid was expelled from York by King Æthelstan, the Anglo-Saxon ruler of England. In 937, Æthelstan won a great victory at Brunanburh over a coalition of Vikings, Scots and Strathclyde Britons led by Gofraid's son Amlaíb:

> Here King Æthelstan, leader of warriors,
> Ring-giver of men, and also his brother,
> The aetheling Edmund, struck life-long glory

'Dublin' in Duffy (ed.), *Medieval Ireland*, p. 135; Angelo Forte, Richard Oram and Frederik Pedersen (eds), *Viking empires* (Cambridge, 2005), pp 69–71; Clare Downham, *Viking kings of Britain and Ireland: the dynasty of Ívarr to AD1014* (Edinburgh, 2007), pp 64–7. **5** *AU*, 934. **6** Clarke, 'Dublin' in Duffy (ed.), *Medieval Ireland*, p. 135. **7** *AU*, 917. **8** Ibid., 919. **9** Ibid., 920, 921.

In strife around Brunanburh, clove the shield wall ...
There the ruler of Northmen, compelled by necessity,
Was put to flight ...
Then the Northmen, bloody survivors of darts,
disgraced in spirit, departed on Ding's Mere,
in nailed boats over deep water,
to seek out Dublin.[10]

Æthelstan died two years after his victory at Brunanburh and the
Scandinavians of York 'belied their pledges, and chose Olaf (Amlaíb) from
Ireland as their king'.[11] Amlaíb son of Gofraid was king of Dublin from 934
until his death in 941. His cousin, Amlaíb Cuarán, was the last king of York
from the Dublin dynasty and he was expelled from York by a Scandinavian
rival in 952.

IRELAND AND THE IRISH IN MEDIEVAL TIMES

The island of Ireland that the grandsons of Ívarr invaded in 914 had a Celtic
and Christian population that was quite distinct from most of its neighbours in Western Europe. The Irish of this time had a flourishing
vernacular culture, preserved today in beautiful manuscripts, skilled metalwork and carved stone high crosses.[12] There were many kings in
tenth-century Ireland, although most were rulers of very small kingdoms.
In other contemporary European countries, they would have been referred
to as duces, earls or jarls. The most powerful Irish kings around the end of
the tenth century were the Northern Uí Néill kings of Cenél nEógain and
Cenél Conaill, the Southern Uí Néill kings of Clann Cholmáin and Brega,

---

10 *ASC*, 937; Darren McGettigan, 'Amlaíb (Óláfr Godfridsson)', *DIB*, 1, pp 96–7; *AU*,
937; Sarah Foot, *Æthelstan: the first king of England* (London, 2011), pp 23–5, 158–85.
11 *ASC*, 941; King Æthelstan died in AD939: *AU*, 939; *Brut Y Tywysogyon*, 939, p. 7.
12 Anthony Lucas, *Treasures of Ireland: Irish pagan and early Christian art* (Dublin,
1973).

the king of Leinster, the king of the Ulaid, the king of Connacht and the Dál Cais and Eóganacht kings of Munster. Until the time of Brian Boru, various Eóganacht dynasties monopolized the kingship of the province. In the tenth century, it was Brian's dynasty, the Dál Cais, that grew very powerful. There was also a high-king of Ireland (often called the king of Tara). Until the beginning of the eleventh century, the high-kingship of the island was confined to the dynasties of the Uí Néill, with the Northern and Southern Uí Néill (by the tenth century usually the kings of Cenél nEógain and Clann Cholmáin) alternating the high-kingship between themselves.[13] The high-kingship of Ireland was a weak institution. By the end of the tenth century, most high-kings from the Cenél nEógain or Clann Cholmáin wielded little authority outside the Uí Néill, and towards the end of their reigns were opposed by the claimant of the succeeding dynasty, who always wished to ensure that a transfer of power took place. The high-kingship 'established no legal rights' and the 'the weakness of Uí Néill polity ... was to prevent them establishing a true monarchy of Ireland'.[14] King Máelsechnaill I of Meath (from the Clann Cholmáin), who was high-king from 846 until his death in 862, was an effective king. He extended his power deep into the southern kingdoms of Leinster and Munster, campaigning and taking hostages in Munster in 854, 856 and 858.[15] Upon his death in 862, AU called Máelsechnaill I 'king of all Ireland'.[16]

The powerful Irish kings *c.*AD1000 lived in well-defended palaces that were important sites on the island. The leading dynasty of the Southern Uí Néill, the Clann Colmáin, had a combined fortress and crannog (a fortified artificial island) complex at Lough Ennell, near Mullingar in Co. Westmeath. The ringfort was called *Dún na Sciath* (the Fort of the Shields), and the crannog was known as *Cró inis Locha Ainninn* (the Island of the House in Lough Ennell).[17] The kings of Cenél nEógain (the leading Northern Uí Néill dynasty) had a palace in the remarkable stone cashel at

---

13 Clare Downham, 'The Vikings in Southern Uí Néill until 1014', *Peritia*, 17–18 (2003–4), 233–55.   **14** Francis John Byrne, *Irish kings and high-kings* (Dublin, 1973), p. 265.   **15** *AU*, 854, 856, 858; Byrne, *Irish kings and high-kings*, pp 262–5.   **16** *AU*, 862.   **17** *AFM*, 932, 1022 (note k); Byrne, *Irish kings and high-kings*, p. 87; Downham, 'The Vikings in Southern Uí Néill', 248.

5 A photograph taken in 1865 of the stone cashel at Aileach, Co. Donegal, the Viking Age palace of the kings of Cenél nEógain (courtesy of the National Library of Ireland).

Aileach, high on a hill at the southern end of the Inishowen Peninsula in Co. Donegal. This stone fort was surrounded by a triple-rampart hillfort dating to the Bronze Age, with a ceremonial road running through the ramparts to the cashel.[18] Aileach was probably the most prestigious royal site in Ireland in the tenth century after the ceremonial centre at Tara. Around the year 1000, the Ua Néill kings of Cenél nEógain began to favour the ringfort at Tullaghoge in the eastern part of their kingdom, from which they could dominate the fertile lands west of Lough Neagh.[19] King Brian and the Dál Cais had their palace at Kincora that was situated on a hill at Killaloe, overlooking the River Shannon.[20]

Below the kings and nobles who formed a substantial part of the Irish population by the end of the tenth century were the freemen, including the *bóaire* (cowman), 'a comfortable and independent farmer'.[21] 'In practice, every freeman was either a lord (*flaith*) or the client (*céle*) of a lord'. Each

18 Elizabeth FitzPatrick, 'Ailech' in Duffy (ed.), *Medieval Ireland*, pp 11–13. **19** James Hogan, 'The Irish law of kingship, with special reference to Ailech and Cenél nEoghain', *PRIA*, 40CI (Dublin, 1931), 205–6. **20** *AFM*, 1010 (note z), 1013; John Bradley, 'Killaloe: a pre-Norman borough?', *Peritia*, 8 (1994), 170–9. **21** Roy Foster (ed.), *The Oxford illustrated history of Ireland* (Oxford, 1991), pp 18–19.

freeman was a landowner with the *céle* or client receiving a loan of cattle from his lord, paying him back with 'interest on his stock' and giving 'the lord political support'.[22] There was also a substantial unfree and slave element to the Irish population. The population of Ireland in the tenth century was overwhelmingly rural, with the majority of kings, nobles and strong farmers living in dispersed ringforts. Ringforts are the most numerous medieval monument in the modern Irish landscape. Forts were small and lightly defended, with either earthen embankments or cashels made of stone (cashels tended to be smaller). Ringforts were used to defend families and livestock from the depredations of wolves and small-scale cattle raiders. It has been suggested that they 'were in fact farmsteads which would have enclosed a single farming family and their retainers'.[23] A cattle-based economy was present all over the island, but evidence of pig husbandry, sheep farming and tillage has also been found. Ringforts close to woodland areas were the most valued, having access to timber for fuel and building purposes and also to the mast (acorns) of oak woods for feeding pigs.[24] The farming and household implements used by the Irish at this time were rich and extensive, a very good range of examples being provided by those excavated by archaeologists from the royal crannog at Lagore in Co. Meath in the 1930s.[25]

While most of Ireland was well settled, there were extensive mountainous and boggy areas that were still wooded and lightly peopled by the year 1000. For example, the Wicklow Mountains in the tenth and eleventh centuries contained large oak woods. Besides Glendalough, in the middle of the mountains, and the territory inhabited by the Fortuatha Laigen dynasty, the region was not fully settled until the Anglo-Norman invasion of Ireland in the twelfth century. The Anglo-Normans drove many of the Irish inhabitants of the plains of Kildare into the mountains. There were further large forested areas in the kingdom of Leinster in the modern

22 Byrne, *Irish kings and high-kings*, p. 28. **23** Matthew Stout, *The Irish ringfort* (Dublin, 1997), pp 32–3. **24** Ibid., pp 35–6, 122. **25** George Eogan, 'Life and living at Lagore' in Alfred Smyth (ed.), *Seanchas: studies in early and medieval Irish archaeology, history and literature in honour of Francis J. Byrne* (Dublin, 2000), pp 67–80.

counties of Wexford, Carlow, Laois and Offaly.[26] Similarly the mountainous regions of west Munster, Connacht and Ulster were heavily forested and lightly peopled in the early eleventh century.[27] In the tenth and eleventh centuries, 'dense herds of fat deer', 'boars or wild woodland pigs', wild cats and wolves, 'rapacious and voracious, [tearing] to pieces cattle and sheep', were present in Ireland and these animals survived on the island into early modern times.[28] Bears (Irish *bethir*, 'a bear, a fierce wild beast') were also present in early medieval Ireland, but they may have died out by AD1000.[29]

Around the year 1000, the Irish people were strongly Christian. The Christian church in Ireland in the late tenth and early eleventh century gave a distinctive character to the population of the island. Christianity in Ireland at this period was monastic and, although there were bishops in the early Irish church, no system of dioceses developed as in much of Western Europe, and hereditary abbots (coarbs) of wealthy monasteries came to lead the Irish church.[30] By the beginning of the eleventh century, the most successful Irish monasteries had sophisticated schools, some master craftsmen and a trading element focused on market days and fairs.[31] The populations of some of the bigger monasteries may have been quite large. The largest and most prestigious monastic centre in Ireland in the year 1000 was Armagh, situated in the eastern marchlands of Cenél nEógain. Armagh was the centre of the medieval cult of St Patrick and claimed primacy over all Ireland; the coarbs of St Patrick who ruled Armagh in the tenth century were mostly from the powerful Clann Sínach family.[32] Every major Irish kingdom had large monasteries. Derry, which lay on the shore of Lough Foyle, was also in the

26 Mark Clinton, 'Settlement patterns in the kingdom of Leinster' in Smyth (ed.), *Seanchas*, p. 296.   **27** John Tierney, 'Wood and woodlands in early medieval Munster' in Michael Monk and John Sheehan (eds), *Early medieval Munster: archaeology, history and society* (Cork, 1998), pp 53–8.   **28** Denis O'Sullivan (ed.), *The natural history of Ireland by Philip O'Sullivan Beare* (Cork, 2009), pp 76–87.   **29** *AFM*, 1404 (note y); Kieran Hickey, *Wolves in Ireland: a natural and cultural history* (Dublin, 2011), p. 14.   **30** Dáibhí Ó Cróinín, 'Conversions to Christianity'; and Martin Holland, 'Twelfth-century church reform' in Duffy (ed.), *Medieval Ireland*, pp 82–5.   **31** Foster (ed.), *The Oxford illustrated history of Ireland*, pp 8–17.   **32** Aubrey Gwynn and R.N. Hadcock, *Medieval religious houses: Ireland* (Dublin, 1970), p. 59.

land of the Cenél nEógain. Clonmacnoise on the east bank of the Shannon, Kells and Clonard were controlled by the kings of Meath during this period, while Kildare and Glendalough were the largest monasteries in Leinster. Emly and Lismore were the main monastic centres in the kingdom of Munster.[33] Command of these monasteries was important to the kings of early eleventh-century Ireland, who often placed family members in control as coarbs. If not closely supervised, the monasteries could become refuges for 'robbers and lawless people', as occurred in Munster in the 980s when King Brian had to expel bandits from Emly, Cork and Lismore.[34]

IRISH AND VIKING WARRIORS

The Irish of this time were also noted as a warlike people with an ancient warrior tradition. In the tenth century and at the beginning of the eleventh, 'the normal Irish fighting man had a spear and a shield'.[35] Spears appear to have been the Irish weapon of choice, with some used for throwing and others for close combat. The medieval Irish had at least twelve different terms to describe them (some of these Irish words for spear included: *sleg*, *manáis*, *láigen*, *goth* and *faobhar*. The Irish word for shield was *sgiath*).[36] Wealthy nobles and kings may have had an expensive well-forged sword (*cloidhem*), possibly of a Roman-influenced native Irish type, with wooden scabbard.[37] The Irish of this period were also noted for not wearing mail shirts or metal helmets into battle. It may even have been an important part of medieval Irish cultural pride not to. Medieval Irish warriors most likely

33 Ibid., pp 28–101; Charles Doherty, Linda Doran and Mary Kelly (eds), *Glendalough: City of God* (Dublin, 2011). **34** *AI*, 987. **35** T.M. Charles-Edwards, 'Irish warfare before 1100' in Thomas Bartlett and Keith Jeffrey (eds), *A military history of Ireland*, p. 27; Andrew Halpin, *Weapons and warfare in Viking and medieval Dublin* (Dublin, 2008), pp 15–21. **36** Andrew Halpin, 'Weapons and warfare in Viking-Age Ireland' in John Sheehan and Donnchadh Ó Corráin (eds), *The Viking age: Ireland and the West, papers from the proceedings of the fifteenth Viking congress* (Dublin, 2010), pp 124–35; Peter Harbison, 'Native Irish arms and armour in medieval Gaelic literature, 1170–1600', *Irish Sword*, 12 (1976), 197–8, 272–6. **37** Etienne Rynne, 'An Irish sword of the 11th century?', *JRSAI*, 92:2 (1962), 208–10.

6 Book of Kells: Irish warrior with spear and shield (detail from fo. 200r, courtesy of the Board of Trinity College Dublin).

wore some form of layered or padded leather armour (the Irish word *erradh* 'war-dress' may have described this type of protective clothing) and some sort of non-metal protective helmet. One Irish word for helmet that was popular in medieval times is *cathbharr*. The main distinguishing feature of the *cathbharr* was 'that it was crested', and some of those worn by kings and nobles may have been elaborately and expensively decorated.[38] Some of the characteristics of tenth-century Irish warfare are recorded in the speech that Niall Glúndub is reputed to have uttered before the Battle of Dublin, fought against the Vikings in 919:

> *Cepe dambáil boccoit breac, agus claideabh leota liach,*
> *Agus gai glass gona troch, téis matar moch do Ath cliath.*

> Whoever wishes for a speckled boss, and a sword of sore-inflicting wounds,
> And a green javelin for wounding wretches, let him go early in the morning to Dublin.[39]

38 *AFM*, 1454; *CGRG*, pp 162–3; Harbison, 'Native Irish arms and armour in medieval Gaelic literature, 1170–1600', 180–94. **39** *AFM*, 917 [*recte* 919].

7 Irish warrior with a possible native-type sword, a figure from the eleventh-century Breac Maedhóc house-shrine (courtesy of the National Museum of Ireland).

As was the case for contemporary Anglo-Saxon armies, Irish warriors 'fought on foot', but may have travelled to the battlefield on horseback.[40] Irish armies of the tenth century do not seem to have had any archers, with volleys of spears or javelins being the missile of choice of the Irish warrior around the year 1000.[41] Despite their shortcomings, Irish armies of this period were very capable when well led, and regularly defeated even large Viking armies throughout the latter half of the tenth century. The Irish warrior was certainly no pushover for his opponent, the mail-clad Viking.

Probably the greatest Irish warrior of the tenth century was Niall Glúndub's son, Muirchertach *na Cochall Craicinn* 'of the Leather Cloaks', who was king of Cenél nEógain and was killed by the Vikings in the year

40 Edwards, 'Irish warfare before 1100', p. 26. **41** Andrew Halpin, 'Weapons and weaponry' in Duffy (ed.), *Medieval Ireland*, pp 511–12; Halpin, 'Weapons and warfare in Viking-Age Ireland', pp 124–35.

8 Book of Kells: Irish horseman (detail from fo. 89r, courtesy of the Board of Trinity College Dublin).

943.[42] Muirchertach's nickname strongly suggests that he favoured traditional Irish forms of armour. Muirchertach was the scourge of the Scandinavians in the north of Ireland, although the Circuit of Ireland for which he is most famous probably never actually took place.[43] *CGRG* builds Brian's most favoured son Murchad up into one of the greatest of Irish warriors. Although Murchad was a capable soldier, the description of him in *CGRG* is most likely fantasy. Indeed, fighting with a large sword in each hand seems very impractical.[44] Tadhg Ua Ceallaigh, the king of Uí Máine, was another highly regarded Irish warrior who fought at Clontarf. The annals contain a record of his successful martial career. In the year 1003, Tadhg inflicted a telling defeat on the Ua Cléirigh branch of the Uí Fiachrach Aidne, which allowed the rival Ua hEidhin family (Brian's in-

42 *AU*, 943.   **43** Donnchadh Ó Corráin, 'Muirchertach Mac Lochlainn and the *Circuit of Ireland*' in Smyth (ed.), *Seanchas*, pp 238–50.   **44** *CGRG*, pp 166–7, 186–9.

9 The Murrough sword fragment: the beautifully decorated remains of a Viking sword hilt found in the vicinity of Wicklow town in the nineteenth century (courtesy of the National Museum of Ireland).

laws) to come to the fore.[45] In some poetry, composed after the battle, Ua Ceallaigh, who was always known after 1014 as *Tadhg Catha Bhriain* (Tadhg of Brian's Battle), is referred to: 'as a wolf-dog pursuing the Danes' (*'Na onchoin a n-diaidh Danmare*).[46]

Brian himself was an accomplished warrior. The ruthless manner in which he defeated and killed all the Munster and Viking kings who had

---

45 *AFM*, 1003. **46** John O'Donovan (ed.), *The tribes and customs of Hy-Many, commonly called O'Kelly's Country* (Dublin, 1843), p. 99; poem relating to Tadhg Ua Ceallaigh and the Clann Ceallaigh, fragment of the Book of Uí Mhaine, *British Library MS Egerton 90*, fo. 19.

10 The Ballinderry Sword: one of the finest Viking swords ever found, discovered during the archaeological excavation of a crannog in Co. Westmeath in 1932. The name of this ninth-century weapon's maker – Ulfbehat of the Rhineland – is inlaid on the blade (courtesy of the National Museum of Ireland).

murdered his brother in the years 977 and 978 is very impressive.[47] Once he became king of Munster, Brian's role was to be a general and strategist. Nevertheless, if the account of his death in *CGRG* is substantially accurate, Brian never forgot how to wield his sword.

Viking warriors were well armed and capable. They were regularly equipped with swords and axes, which were regarded as prestigious weapons. Well made and expensive, the Scandinavians often gave individual names to these weapons.[48] Vikings were also known to use spears and bows and arrows, and even to throw stones in battle.[49] To defend themselves, the Viking soldiers wore rounded metal helmets with nose and neck guards and shirts of mail, and carried large round shields that were often painted in bright colours. The mail shirts stretched from the neck to the knee and were worn over padded undergarments. Many of the nobles in Viking armies wore a mail shirt, although the extent of mail armour

47 *AI*, 977, 978.   **48** Halpin, *Weapons and warfare in Viking and medieval Dublin*, pp 152–62.   **49** Else Roesdahl, *The Vikings* (London, 1998), pp 142–4.

11 A selection of artefacts from Viking Dublin, including woodwork decorated in a local version of Scandnavian Ringerike style, red and green porphyry fragments from Rome, a piece of Baltic amber and a gold ring and bracelet (courtesy of the National Museum of Ireland).

being worn by entire Scandinavian armies is uncertain.[50] Viking warriors also rode to battle on horseback but then dismounted to fight on foot. Of course it was the long sleek warships that carried large numbers of raiders ashore for which the Vikings were most noted and feared in medieval times.[51]

Vikings of the tenth and early eleventh centuries and earlier times were adventurous, aggressive and very talented warriors. Irish kings when facing Viking armies in battle had constantly to be on their guard for tricks and battle ploys. A favoured Viking tactic was to hide a large portion of their army in a wood or defile, and then to emerge from cover during the battle to take their enemies by surprise in the flank or rear. Although very little is

50 Ibid., pp 143–4; Jim Bradbury, *The Routledge companion to medieval warfare* (London, 2004), pp 254, 257–8. **51** Roesdahl, *The Vikings*, pp 85–8; The Viking Ship Museum, *Welcome on board! The Sea Stallion from Glendalough: a Viking longship recreated* (Roskilde, 2007); Mary Valante, 'Viking kings and Irish fleets during Dublin's Viking Age' in Bradley, Fletcher and Simms (eds), *Dublin in the medieval world*, pp 73–82; M.K. Lawson, *Cnut: England's Viking king, 1016–35* (Stroud, 1993/2011), pp 223–4.

12 The remains of the Viking longship Skuldelev 2. This large and imposing warship was made from trees felled near Dublin in the summer of 1042 (© the Viking Ship Museum in Roskilde, Denmark. Photograph by Werner Karrasch).

known about him, the Scandinavian leader Tuirgéis, who was killed by the king of Meath in 845, may have been one of the most powerful early Vikings who raided in Ireland.[52] The grandsons of Ívarr who invaded Ireland in the year 914 and campaigned extensively on the island for the next decade were also highly successful warriors. Sitric Silkenbeard, the Hiberno-Norse king of Dublin at the time of Clontarf, does not appear to have been much of a soldier. In his major battles with Brian, he let his

52 *AU*, 845.

13 The *Sea Stallion from Glendalough*, a recreation of the Viking warship Skuldelev 2, off the coast of Co. Wicklow in 2007 (© the Viking Ship Museum in Roskilde, Denmark. Photograph by Werner Karrasch).

brothers and nephews do all the fighting. Although Sitric was a capable king of Dublin, being shrewd, ambitious and ruthless, he does not appear to have inspired much confidence in his fighting men. This may have contributed to the series of heavy defeats that the Dublinmen suffered at the hands of the Irish in the years leading up to Clontarf.

THE HIBERNO-NORSE

By the early eleventh century, the towns along the Irish coast inhabited by the foreigners had grown very wealthy through trade. These were Dublin, Waterford, Limerick and Cork, which were founded by Vikings raiders of

villages of Wicklow (possibly *Uíkar-Ló*, meadow of the bay) and Arklow (possibly *Arnketill-Ló*, Arnketill's meadow), which lay to the south of Dublin at the mouths of rivers that flow into the Irish Sea, may also have been included as being part of the shire of Dublin, the entire coastline is unlikely to have been.[64] Most of coastal Wicklow around ADI000 was still inhabited by minor Irish dynasties from the kingdom of Leinster. Small areas around the towns of Waterford, Limerick and Cork were also settled by the Hiberno-Norse. Wexford (*Ueigs-Fjorðr*, Fjord of Ueig) in south Leinster was also an important Scandinavian settlement. Remains of Dublin-style houses have been found there and a substantial Hiberno-Norse population also lived in the surrounding countryside.[65] The Vikings of Limerick were unrelated to the grandsons of Ívarr and this led to warfare between the town and the Vikings of Dublin and Waterford throughout the 920s and 930s.[66]

By the beginning of the eleventh century, the inhabitants of the Viking towns of Ireland, owing to their interaction with the native Irish, had developed their own distinctive Hiberno-Norse culture. The houses in Dublin and Waterford were constructed in an unusual Scandinavian style, and eventually the Vikings in Ireland also appear to have become Christian.[67] Amlaíb Cuarán became a Christian during the 940s at the prompting of Edmund, king of the English. Although Amlaíb renounced his new religion for a time, he died as a Christian in 981, in exile in Iona, the island monastery off the coast of Scotland.[68] The Hiberno-Norse of the Irish towns grew very wealthy through trade with the native Irish, but they could still be dangerous and destructive Viking raiders when the opportunity

1997), pp 177–9.   **64** Colmán Etchingham, 'Evidence of Scandinavian settlement in Wicklow' in Ken Hannigan and William Nolan (eds), *Wicklow: history and society* (Dublin, 1994), pp 113–35; Clinton, 'Settlement patterns in the kingdom of Leinster', pp 290–4; Colmán Etchingham, 'The Viking impact on Glendalough' in Doherty, Doran and Kelly (eds), *Glendalough: City of God*, pp 211–22.   **65** Clinton, 'Settlement patterns in the kingdom of Leinster', p. 294.   **66** Downham, *Viking kings of Britain and Ireland*, pp 35–42.   **67** Lesley Abrams, 'The conversion of the Scandinavians of Dublin', *Anglo-Norman Studies*, 20 (1997), 1–29.   **68** Darren McGettigan, 'Amlaíb (Óláfr) Cuarán', *DIB*, 1, pp 97–8; Alex Woolf, 'Amlaíb Cuarán and the Gael, 941–81' in Seán Duffy (ed.), *Medieval Dublin*, 3 (Dublin, 2001), pp 34–43.

presented itself. In the year 942, 'the heathens of Áth Cliath' plundered the monasteries of Kildare and Clonmacnoise in the kingdoms of Leinster and Meath.[69] Eight years later, the Vikings of Dublin caused great destruction to the monastery at Slane in the kingdom of Brega when they destroyed many of the treasures of the monastery and also burnt some of the monastic community alive.[70] In 951, they plundered the wealthy monastery at Kells in the kingdom of Meath. From this base, the Viking raiders proceeded to attack many more monastic sites in Meath. In total, 'three thousand men or more were taken captive and a great spoil of cattle and horses and gold and silver was taken away' in what must have been a disastrous raid on the kingdom of the Southern Uí Néill.[71] Even as late as the year 995, Sitric Silkenbeard raided the monastery of Downpatrick near the coast in the kingdom of the Ulaid.[72] Naturally, such actions created great fear among the Irish of being captured by a Viking raiding party and sold off at Dublin into slavery. The churchmen of the monasteries of Ireland must also have lived in constant fear of attack without warning by Viking raiders. For their part, the Vikings must have been in terror of being killed and beheaded by Irish warriors if caught and defeated while on a raid.

Once the initial Scandinavian raids were over and the Vikings began to settle in towns, 'contacts between the native Irish and the foreigners were fairly common and often far from hostile'.[73] Both the Irish and the Hiberno-Norse adopted loan words and personal names from each others' languages and, by the year 1000, there was extensive intermarriage between the Irish and the Scandinavian royal families.[74] For example, Brian Boru's daughter Sláine married King Sitric Silkenbeard of Dublin (and they had at least three sons together).[75] Similarly, King Máelsechnaill II of Meath married a sister of King Sitric called 'Maelmaire daughter of Amlaíb' (Cuarán).[76] Perhaps the best-known example of intermarriage between the

69 *AU*, 942. **70** Ibid., 950. **71** Ibid., 951. **72** Ibid., 995. **73** Brian Ó Cuív, 'Personal names as an indicator of relations between native Irish and settlers in the Viking period' in Bradley (ed.), *Settlement and society in medieval Ireland*, pp 85–6. **74** Diarmaid Ó Muirithe, *From the Viking word-hoard: a dictionary of Scandinavian words in the languages of Britain and Ireland* (Dublin, 2010), pp xx–xxix. **75** Howard Clarke, 'Sitriuc Silkbeard', *DIB*, 8, pp 974–7. **76** *AFM*, 1021.

Irish and the Hiberno-Norse is that of Gormlaith, the daughter of the Leinster king Murchad (d. 972) of the Uí Fáeláin dynasty (the kings of Naas). Gormlaith married Amlaíb Cuarán, the Hiberno-Norse king of Dublin, and Sitric Silkenbeard was their son. Some time after King Amlaíb died in 981, Gormlaith married the high-king Máelsechnaill II of Meath, whom she appears to have divorced. Gormlaith married a third time and this time her husband was Brian Boru. Gormlaith was the mother of Brian's prominent son Donnchadh. At some stage, Brian and Gormlaith also divorced.[77] A stanza of poetry in the Book of Leinster has Gormlaith's many marriages as its theme. It states:

> *Trí lémend ra ling Gormlaith,*
> *ní lingfea ben co bráth;*
> *léim i nÁth Cliath, léim i Temraig,*
> *léim i Cassel, carnmaig ós chách.*

Three leaps did Gormlaith perform which no other woman shall do till Doomsday: a leap into Dublin, a leap into Tara, a leap into Cashel, the plain with the mound which surpasses all.[78]

Amlaíb Cuarán, although a Hiberno-Norse king, was patron to the tenth-century Meath poet, Cináed Ua hArtacáin, who, when he died in 975, was called 'chief poet of Ireland' and 'chief poet of the northern half of Ireland'.[79] Ua hArtacáin is said to have composed the poem 'Achall' (a poem about the Hill of Skreen near Tara) for King Amlaíb, who rewarded the Irish poet with the gift of a prized horse.[80] In one stanza, Ua hArtacáin records this reward for his poetry from the king of Dublin:

77 Ailbhe MacShamhráin, 'Gormlaith', *DIB*, 4, pp 158–9. **78** Ó Cuív, 'Personal names as an indicator of relations between native Irish and settlers in the Viking period', p. 86; Anne O'Sullivan (ed.), *The Book of Leinster, formerly Lebor na Núa chongbála*, 6 (Dublin, 1983), p. 1462. **79** *AU*, 975; *AT*, 974 [*recte* 975]; *AFM*, 973 [*recte* 975]; Aidan Breen, 'Cináed Ua hArtacáin', *DIB*, 9, pp 588–9; Dermot Gleeson and Seán MacAirt, 'The Annals of Roscrea', *PRIA*, 59C3 (1958), 171. **80** Edward Gwynn (ed.), *The Metrical Dindsenchas*, I (Dublin, 1903), pp 46–53, notes p. 80.

Amlaib Átha Cliath cétaig
rogab rígi i mBeind Etair,
tallus lúag mo dúane de,
ech d'echaib ána Aichle.

Amlaíb of Dublin the hundred-strong,
who gained the kingship of Howth;
I bore off from him as price of my song
a horse of the horses of Achall.[81]

THE UÍ NÉILL HIGH-KINGS

The Irish kings were quite successful in fighting the Scandinavians. The complex nature of Irish kingship and the multitude of small kingdoms on the island ensured that there was no quick conquest of Ireland by the Vikings, as occurred in Anglo-Saxon England in the ninth century and in 1013 and 1016. Nevertheless, the Viking threat to the Irish was still very serious at times; for example, after 914, when it appeared that the grandsons of Ívarr might succeed in conquering the entire island. The leaders of the Irish in the early Viking wars were the kings of the Northern and Southern Uí Néill, particularly the kings of Clann Cholmáin and Cenél nEógain. Máelsechnaill I, the king of Meath and high-king of Ireland from 846 until his death in 862, was the first major Irish king to oppose the Vikings in Ireland.[82] In 845, AU record that he captured the Viking leader called Tuirgéis and had him drowned in Lough Owel.[83] In 848, Máelsechnaill was victorious in a major battle against the Scandinavians 'in which seven hundred fell',[84] and in 856 it was recorded that there was 'great warfare between the heathens and Máelsechnaill'.[85]

The most noteworthy fighters against the Vikings in Ireland were the kings of the Northern Uí Néill dynasty, the Cenél nEógain. Áed Findliath

---

81 Ibid., pp 52–3. **82** Byrne, *Irish kings and high-kings*, p. 263. **83** *AU*, 845.
84 Ibid., 848. **85** Ibid., 856.

of Cenél nEógain, 'whom spear-point could not conquer' (*na ra buadad rind*) was high-king of Ireland from 862 until his death in 879.[86] He was very successful against Scandinavian settlements in the north of Ireland.[87] This was even though Áed allied himself in 861–2 to the Vikings of Dublin (he married his daughter to the king of Dublin) in order to ensure his succession to the high-kingship.[88] AU record that in 866, 'Áed son of Niall plundered all the strongholds of the foreigners, that is in the territory of the north, both in Cenél nEógain and Dál nAraide', and 'took away their heads, their flocks and their herds'.[89] In a major engagement on Lough Foyle, Áed's army killed over two hundred Vikings.[90] Áed's son and heir, Niall Glúndub, was high-king of Ireland from 916 to 919. Niall led the Irish resistance to the invasion of the island by the grandsons of Ívarr. Although from the Cenél nEógain dynasty, Niall campaigned against the Vikings in the southern kingdoms of Ireland. In 917, he led an army composed of contingents from the Northern and Southern Uí Néill into Munster 'to make war on the heathens'.[91] Once there, Niall encamped against the Viking army for twenty days. In 919, Niall Glúndub and the cream of his army, including the kings of Connacht and Brega, were killed by the grandsons of Ívarr at the Battle of Dublin 'i.e. of Cill Mosamhóg, by the side of Áth Cliath' that was fought on 14 September that year.[92] Such was the success of the Viking army in Ireland at this time and the carnage at the Battle of Dublin, that a poem inserted in AFM associated with the battle speaks of *Dergus ár nGoedhell dar rian*, 'A red slaughter of the Gael in every path'.[93]

86 R.A. Stewart MacAlister (ed.), *Lebor Gabála Erenn: The book of the taking of Ireland*, 5 (Dublin, 1956), pp 552–3. **87** Byrne, *Irish kings and high-kings*, p. 266; Ann Hamlin, 'The early church in Tyrone to the twelfth century' in Charles Dillon and Henry Jefferies (eds), *Tyrone: history and society* (Dublin, 2000), pp 96–7. **88** Darren McGettigan and Ailbhe MacShamhráin, 'Áed Findliath', *DIB*, 1, pp 32–3; Valante, *The Vikings in Ireland*, pp 92–4. **89** *AU*, 866; Ailbhe MacShamhráin, 'The making of Tír nEógain: Cenél nEógain and the Airgialla from the sixth to the eleventh centuries' in Dillon and Jefferies (eds), *Tyrone: history and society*, p. 79. **90** *AU*, 866. **91** Ibid., 917. **92** Ibid., 919; *AFM*, 917 [*recte* 919]; John O'Donovan believed that this battle took place at 'Mosamhog's Church, now Kilmashoge, near Rathfarnham': ibid., note n. **93** *AFM*, 917 [*recte* 919].

As we have seen, Niall Glúndub's son Muirchertach, who was nicknamed *na Cochall Craicinn* 'of the Leather Cloaks' and was king of Cenél nEógain from 938, was another great Irish warrior.[94] From the time in 921 when he defeated a raiding force of Scandinavians, which was fanning out north after the Viking seizure of the monastic centre of Armagh, Muirchertach was an unceasing opponent of the Vikings in the north of Ireland.[95] In numerous skirmishes and small battles, Muirchertach's army killed hundreds of Vikings, until in 938 he besieged the town of Dublin itself and plundered its hinterland.[96] Muirchertach even survived being captured by the Vikings in 939. In that year, a small Scandinavian force in a daring raid sailed into Lough Foyle and sacked the palace of Aileach, capturing Muirchertach in the process.[97] Muirchertach 'ransomed himself afterwards', before he was carried away by the longships to Dublin.[98] He was eventually killed by the Scandinavians in February 943 defending the road from the coast to Armagh.[99] His son Domnall Ua Néill, who was high-king of Ireland from 956 to 980, continued to fight the Vikings in the north, with success. In 945, utilizing the opportunity presented by the icy conditions that froze the lakes of Ireland that year, his army crossed the ice to wipe out a troublesome band of Vikings based on Lough Neagh. Domnall also destroyed their ships that must have become trapped.[1] This Scandinavian colony on Lough Neagh may have been established in the year 930 by a jarl called Torulb, who was killed in 932 by Domnall's father.[2]

Unfortunately for the kings of Cenél nEógain, their very success in expelling the Vikings from their shoreline put future kings of the northern kingdom at a disadvantage in comparison to rival kings from Leinster, Meath and Munster. This was because once the Viking towns in the south became wealthy trading centres they became vulnerable to control by the southern kings. Overlordship of a Hiberno-Norse town greatly increased

94 Ó Corráin, 'Muirchertach Mac Lochlainn and the *Circuit of Ireland'*, pp 238–50. **95** *AU*, 921. **96** Ibid., 926, 933, 938. **97** Ibid., 939. **98** Ibid. **99** Ibid., 943. **1** Ibid., 945; *CS*, [944]. **2** *AU*, 930, 932; *AFM*, 928, 930; Valante, *The Vikings in Ireland*, p. 107.

the power of an Irish king, through levies of tribute and the contributions of heavily armed warriors and fleets of Scandinavian warships.[3] But for their success, the kings of Cenél nEógain might have controlled Hiberno-Norse towns on the shores of Lough Foyle and Lough Neagh. By the beginning of the eleventh century, the nearest Scandinavian town to the Cenél nEógain was Dublin. Nevertheless, a later medieval Irish poet still referred to the dynasty at this period as being 'like raging lions, the kings of [Cenél] nEógain over Ireland' (*mar leomain luind rígrad Eogain ós Érind*).[4]

---

3 Byrne, *Irish kings and high-kings*, p. 268.   **4** Stewart MacAlister (ed.), *Lebor Gabála Erenn*, 5, pp 558–9.

2 Brian seizes the high-kingship

Domnall Ua Néill the high-king of Ireland died in 980.[1] His successor as high-king was to prove to be one of the most successful of all the kings from the Uí Néill; this was Máelsechnaill II of Clann Cholmáin. Máelsechnaill II was a highly respected high-king. A jewel-encrusted *carracan* or model of the Temple of Solomon he gifted to the monastery of Clonmacnoise was preserved for over a century on the altar of the great church there.[2] From the entries for the year 980 in AU and AI, it appears that he was attacked immediately when he became high-king, by Amlaíb Cuarán, the Hiberno-Norse king of Dublin. Amlaíb sent a large force of Viking warriors from 'Áth Cliath and the Isles' under the command of his son Ragnall to attack Máelsechnaill, perhaps even as the king of Meath was being inaugurated as high-king, as the ensuing battle took place on the hill of Tara.[3] The battle that followed was a fierce encounter in which Máelsechnaill II was victorious 'and very great slaughter was inflicted on the foreigners therein, and foreign power [was ejected] from Ireland'.[4] The commanders of the Viking army, Ragnall mac Amlaíb and Conamal, the son of a Hiberno-Norse sub-king, were killed. AI record 'a measuring rod being required everywhere' to count the number of Viking dead.[5] In 983, Máelsechnaill defeated the king of Leinster, Domnall Clóen, in battle, killing one of the Leinsterman's Hiberno-Norse mercenaries, Gilla Pátraic mac Ímair the son of the king of Waterford.[6] Entries in a number of less reliable annals for the years 981, 989 and 994 state that Máelsechnaill II captured Dublin on three occasions, when he released thousands of Irish slaves, placed a tax of 'an ounce of gold for every garden, on Christmas night, forever', and took 'the ring of Tomar and the sword of Carlus … from the foreigners of Áth Cliath'.[7] When Máelsechnaill released the slaves from Dublin, he is reputed to have stated:

---

1 *AU*, 980; *AI*, 980. 2 *AFM*, 1129. 3 Downham, *Viking kings of Britain and Ireland*, pp 266–7. 4 *AU*, 980. 5 *AI*, 980. 6 *AU*, 983; Downham, *Viking kings of Britain and Ireland*, pp 252, 260–1. 7 *AFM*, 979 [*recte* 980/1], 988 [*recte* 989], 994.

cech aen do Gaoidhealaibh fil hi ccrich Gall i ndaeire 7 dochraide taed as dia thír fodhesin frí sidh 7 subha.

Everyone of the Gael who is in the territory of the foreigners, in servitude and bondage, let him go to his own territory in peace and happiness.[8]

Máelsechnaill II first took notice of Brian Boru (Brian was known as Bórumha after a Dál Cais fortress, *Béal Bóramha*, the port of the cattle-tribute, which lay on the River Shannon, north of Kincora) in the year 982 when Brian, as king of Munster, sent his army to raid the kingdom of Osraige (modern day Co. Kilkenny and west Co. Laois).[9] Osraige was a border kingdom between Munster and Leinster that Máelsechnaill regarded as being within his sphere of influence.[10] In retaliation, King Máelsechnaill invaded the heartland of Brian's kingdom in north Munster and symbolically destroyed 'the Tree of Mag Adar', a sacred tree that grew at the inauguration site of the Dál Cais at Magh Adair in the parish of Clooney, in modern Co. Clare.[11] This act sent a message to Brian and the Dál Cais to respect the traditions of kingship in Ireland that favoured the Uí Néill. By 982, Máelsechnaill II recognized that Brian Boru was the most powerful king in Munster and a leader to be monitored and watched. The high-king from Meath knew that Brian had risen to prominence very quickly through the power of revenge. In 976, Brian's brother Mathgamain, the king of Cashel, was 'treacherously' killed by rival kings in Munster.[12] The next year, Brian killed Ímar the Viking king of Limerick and his two sons who were implicated in the death of Mathgamain, as well as killing all the Viking mercenaries who were living among the Uí Fidhgeinte, the

---

8 Ibid., 979 [*recte* 980/1]; Holm, 'The slave trade of Dublin', 332; Downham, 'The Vikings in Southern Uí Néill', 241–2. **9** John O'Donovan (ed.), 'The *Circuit* of Ireland by Muircertach Mac Neill, prince of Aileach; a poem written in the year 942 by Cormacan Eigeas, chief poet of the north of Ireland', *Tracts relating to Ireland*, 1 (Dublin, 1841), contains very good notes on prominent places surrounding Kincora such as Béal Bóramha on pp 45–7. **10** *AI*, 982. **11** Ibid.; *AFM*, 981 [*recte* 982], 1051, 1599 (note y); Anthony Lucas, 'The sacred trees of Ireland', *JCHAS*, 68 (1963), 16–54; 'Magh Adhair: a ritual and inauguration complex in south-east Clare', *Archaeology Ireland: heritage guide*, 2 (1998). **12** *AI*, 976; *AU*, 976.

people of King Donnubán, the king who had first captured Mathgamain.[13] In 978, Brian killed the man who had had his brother 'put to death', Máel Muad son of Bran king of Desmond (AI give him the title 'king of Cashel'). Máel Muad was killed at a battle fought at Belach Lechta near Macroom.[14]

THE DÁL CAIS

The high-king Máelsechnaill II must have noted Brian's modest dynastic heritage. Brian's ancestors were the Uí Toirdealbaig, a branch of a minor Munster dynasty called In Déis Becc. The lands of In Déis Becc lay to the north and south of the Shannon in modern Co. Clare and the southeast of Co. Limerick. The Uí Toirdealbaig dynasty was part of the northern section of In Déis Becc, called In Déis Tuaiscirt. The original lands of the Uí Toirdealbaig lay in the 'great natural fortress at Killaloe'.[15] Brian's family rose to prominence as the defenders of In Déis Tuaiscirt from the Vikings who settled in Limerick, whose town was built on land taken from In Déis Tuaiscirt in the early tenth century.[16] The Vikings in Limerick were quite powerful and regarded the River Shannon as their natural hinterland. In 922, the Viking leader Tomrair son of Elgi, 'Jarl of the foreigners of Limerick', raided up the Shannon and plundered Clonmacnoise and the kingdom of Meath.[17] Brian's grandfather Lorcán was the first prominent member of his family. The death of Brian's father Cennétig in the year 951 is noted in AI, where he is called 'rígdamna of Cashel' (*ríoghdhamhna*, medieval Irish for one eligible for kingship).[18] It was Brian's brother Mathgamain who solidly established the family as a power to be reckoned with in Munster. In 967, he defeated the Vikings of Limerick at the Battle of Sulchuait, burning down their town the following morning.[19]

---

13 *AI*, 977. **14** Ibid., 978; *AU*, 978; *AFM*, 976 [*recte* 978] (notes e, k). **15** John Ryan, 'The Dalcassians', *North Munster Antiquarian Journal* (1943), 191–202. **16** Ibid., pp 189–203; Byrne, *Irish kings and high-kings*, pp 180–2; E.P. Kelly and Edmond O'Donovan, 'A Viking longphort near Athlunkard, Co. Clare', *Archaeology Ireland*, 12:4 (1998), 13–16. **17** *AI*, 922. **18** Ibid., 951; Simms, *From kings to warlords*, p. 177. **19** *AI*, 967; *AU*, 967.

To impress their rivals, the Uí Toirdealbaig adopted the dynastic name *Dál Cais*, which meant 'the seed of [an ancestor figure named] Cas'. Although a new invention, this was an old-fashioned term used in earlier centuries. The Uí Toirdealbaig justified their seizure of the kingship of Munster by manipulating and altering the memory of a type of alternating kingship called *selaidecht* that had once existed between the kings of In Déis Tuaiscirt and In Déis Deiscirt. Brian's family changed the kingdom mentioned from In Déis Becc to the kingship of Munster (Cashel) that would now alternate between the Dál Cais and the Eóganacht, the traditional ruling dynasties of Munster. This was a blatant forgery.[20] Mathgamain was the first king of Munster from the Dál Cais and Brian was the second. Although the Eóganacht Chaisil inflicted a severe defeat on the Dál Cais in 944, when two of Mathgamain and Brian's elder brothers, Find and Dub, were killed at the Battle of Gort Rotacháin, Mathgamain himself did not initially experience much resistance from the Eóganacht.[21] The high-king Máelsechanill II must have noted the great success of the Dál Cais and perhaps thought that the rise of such an obscure family to major prominence was very unusual.

To combat the Vikings in Limerick, Brian's grandfather and father must have worked hard at improving the capabilities of the force of warriors the Dál Cais could put into the field against their enemies. Certainly by the time Mathgamain and Brian became kings of Munster their warriors were very capable and proved able to defeat their Viking and Eóganacht opponents, almost at will. Brian appears to have carried these developments a step further. As king of Munster, Brian hired large forces of mercenaries to add to his army. AI record that in 985 the Déisi who ruled most of modern Co. Waterford 'raided Brian's mercenaries and took three hundred cows'.[22] Brian's brother Mathgamain also had a commander of mercenaries called Cathal son of Fogartach, who, when he was killed on a raid in 968,

---

20 Ryan, 'The Dalcassians', 191–4; Byrne, *Irish kings and high-kings*, pp 11, 180. **21** *AU*, 944; *CS*, [943]; M.A. O'Brien (ed.), *Corpus Genealogiarum Hiberniae*, 1 (Dublin, 1962), p. 237; Donnchadh Ó Corráin, 'Caithréim Chellacháin Chaisil', *Ériu*, 25 (1974), 1–70. **22** *AI*, 985; Simms, *From kings to warlords*, pp 117–18.

was given the title 'royal mercenary of Ireland' (*rí-amus Herend*).[23] By 1014, Brian must have had substantial numbers of mercenaries in his service. He quickly quelled the revolt of the Déisi in 985. Their king was chased into the Scandinavian town of Waterford and 'the whole of the Déisi' was plundered.[24] As king of Munster, Brian was very careful to keep tight control of the sub-kings and Hiberno-Norse towns of his kingdom. In 986, he imprisoned his nephew, Mathgamain's son Áed, to ensure that there was no dynastic trouble among his close family.[25] In 987, Brian led an expedition 'across Desmond', when he took the hostages of the monastic centres of Cork, Lismore and Emly 'as a guarantee of the banishment of robbers and lawless people there-from'.[26] There was also trouble in 990 when Ímar the Viking king of Waterford fled from Brian.[27] This was the extent of the internal unrest in the kingdom of Munster during Brian's reign as king. The peace and stability of Munster during his reign made the kingdom prosperous and powerful, allowing Brian to make his bid for the high-kingship of the entire island.

THE COLLAPSE OF THE OLD HIGH-KINGSHIP

Traditionally, the kings of Munster were not so powerful as the Uí Néill high-kings. Even so, the high-king Máelsechnaill I, who reigned in the mid-ninth century, was the only Uí Néill high-king who managed to extend his power into Munster to any real extent. The Eóganacht king of Munster, however, Cormac mac Cuilennáin, had been quite powerful at the beginning of the tenth century. Brian Boru was never a king to lack ambition. It is unclear exactly when or why he decided to challenge the Uí Néill for the high-kingship of Ireland. His family was a highly ambitious dynasty, which strove to increase its power and status in each succeeding generation, with a definite disregard for long established custom and tradition. As such, Brian's bid for the high-kingship was the logical next step for his family. Brian was to follow this path with talent and determination.

23 *AI*, 968. **24** Ibid., 985. **25** Ibid., 986. **26** Ibid., 987. **27** Ibid., 990.

Brian began the challenge to Máelsechnaill II by raiding into the kingdoms of Connacht and Leinster and taking the hostages of any kings who would submit to him. He did this in the years 983, 984, 988, 990, 991, 993 and 996.[28] Brian made good use of fleets of ships in these attacks and allied himself with Viking raiders on occasion, when he had use of their assistance.[29] AI indicate that Brian's fleets were often quite large. Brian's forces also raided the kingdom of Meath from Lough Ree in 988.[30] Máelsechnaill II naturally fought back against the Munster army. In 983, when he defeated the king of Leinster in battle, the Gilla Pátraic and his soldiers killed by the warriors of the high-king may have been a force of Hiberno-Norse from the town of Waterford left in Leinster by Brian to assist the Leinstermen.[31] Máelsechnaill also counter-raided into Connacht.[32] AU record that in 990 the high-king defeated the forces of Munster at the Battle of Carn Fordroma.[33] It is Brian's persistence over these years that appears to have worn Máelsechnaill down. The constant raids into the high-king's vassal kingdoms must have been very unsettling, coupled with the fact that no king of Munster had ever really done anything like this before. Máelsechnaill II was a pragmatic and sensible king. As a result, in 997 he held a royal conference with Brian 'and they divided Ireland between them into two'. Máelsechnaill was given *Leth Cuinn*, the traditional northern half of Ireland (the kingdoms of Meath, Connacht and the North), while Brian was awarded *Leth Moga*, the traditional southern half of the island (the kingdoms of Munster, Leinster and Dublin).[34] This appears to have been a workable solution to the rivalry between Brian and Máelsechnaill and it ushered in a period of cooperation between the two kings. In 997, Máelsechnaill gave the hostages of Leinster that he held over to Brian and the next year both kings marched on the Hiberno-Norse town of Dublin and took hostages from the Scandinavians 'to ensure good behaviour towards the Irish'.[35] The following year, in a further gesture of

---

28 Ibid., 983, 984, 988, 991, 993, 996.   29 Ibid., 983, 984, 988, 993.   30 Ibid., 988.
31 *AU*, 983.   32 Ibid., 985, 992.   33 Ibid., 990.   34 *AI*, 997.   35 Ibid.; *AU*, 998.
36 *AI*, 998.

goodwill, Brian handed over the hostages of the kingdom of Connacht to Máelsechnaill after gathering them 'in one week'.[36]

In 999, Brian faced the first serious threat to his ambition when the Hiberno-Norse of the wealthy town of Dublin decided to oppose him. The Hiberno-Norse of Dublin had been the traditional enemies of the Uí Néill high-kings. When Brian became their overlord, the king of Dublin, Sitric Silkenbeard, may have decided to test his abilities and determination. The Hiberno-Norse of Dublin may also have been unsettled by the large-scale Viking invasions of Anglo-Saxon England that occurred throughout the 990s and Sitric may have decided that he did not want any Irish overlord. Sitric took prisoner and deposed the king of Leinster and placed his uncle Máelmórda of the Uí Fáelán dynasty in his place.[37] When Brian met the combined Viking–Leinster army in battle at Glenn Máma in the western foothills of the Wicklow Mountains, the Dubliners and their allies were heavily defeated.[38] King Sitric's brother Aralt and an Irish ally, Cuilén son of Étigén, were both killed in the battle.[39] Early twentieth-century local tradition places this major engagement at the Blackhill near Dunlavin, where 'old people in the area remembered human bones being found in the valley'.[40] According to some poetry preserved in AFM, the fighting took place 'Around the stone at *Claen Conghair* (the slope of the troop)' and the defeated warriors from the Viking–Leinster army fled 'northwards' through a nearby forest.[41] Brian may have brought only his best warriors to fight at Glenn Máma, since AI refer to his army as 'the choice troops' of Munster.[42]

The Munster army fell upon a defenceless Dublin, expelled King Sitric and burned the wood of Tomar that was sacred to the Dublin Scandinavians.[43] The impact of the fall of Dublin at this time was felt all around the Irish Sea. The Welsh Chronicle of the Princes records that in

37 *AU*, 999. **38** Grogan and Kilfeather (eds), *Archaeological inventory of County Wicklow*, p. 205. **39** *AU*, 999; *AI*, 999; Downham, *Viking kings of Britain and Ireland*, pp 245, 250; Ailbhe MacShamhráin, 'Brian Bóruma, Armagh and high kingship', *Seanchas Ard Mhacha*, 20:2 (2005), 9. **40** Grogan and Kilfeather (eds), *Archaeological inventory of County Wicklow*, p. 205. **41** *AFM*, 998 [*recte* 999] (note a). **42** *AI*, 999. **43** Ailbhe MacShamhráin, 'The Battle of Glen Máma, Dublin, and the high-kingship of Ireland: a millennial commemoration' in Seán Duffy (ed.), *Medieval Dublin*, 2 (Dublin, 2001), pp 53–64. **44** *Brut Y Tywysogyon*, 999–1000, p. 11.

this year 'the Irish ravaged Dublin'.[44] Despite his expulsion, Sitric Silkenbeard soon agreed a comprehensive deal with Brian and was allowed to return to his town. The Dublin ruler possibly agreed to marry the king of Munster's daughter Sláine at this time and then 'handed over his hostages' and was re-installed by Brian 'in the fort of the foreigners'.[45] Although Sitric became Brian's son-in-law, this fact did not ensure loyalty to Brian on the part of the king of Dublin when a major crisis eventually erupted in 1013. Brian attempted to build on the success of his capture of Dublin by invading the kingdom of Meath, but he was defeated by Máelsechnaill. An advance force on horseback that he sent on ahead of his army from Dublin and Leinster was almost wiped out by Máelsechnaill's soldiers.[46] This act indicated to King Máelsechnaill that the period of co-kingship with Brian was at an end and that Brian clearly had ambitions to be king of more than merely the southern half of Ireland (*Leth Moga*). The period of cooperation between the two kings had lasted only three years.

Máelsechnaill made extensive preparations to oppose Brian. In 1001, the king of Meath built 'a great obstruction' at Athlone on the River Shannon to prevent the Munster fleet from sailing into Lough Ree.[47] A raiding force from Munster was also forced back over the southern border of the kingdom of Meath.[48] Nevertheless, when Brian returned with the Munster army in 1002, Máelsechnaill's resistance collapsed and he gave hostages from his kingdom to Brian. The king of Connacht yielded hostages at the same time.[49] This was a historic event on the island. Never before had an Uí Néill high-king abdicated his kingship and yielded hostages to the king of Munster. For a king such as Máelsechnaill II, who was evidently very capable, to have had to do so is indicative of Brian Boru's superior talents.

The saga account of King Brian's life, Cogadh Gaedhel re Gallaibh, contains an interesting tale of how Northern Uí Néill support for Máelsechnaill failed to materialize. *CGRG* states that Brian's army marched to Tara, the ceremonial centre of the Uí Néill high-kingship, and sent messengers to Máelsechnaill II 'and they demanded hostages from him, or

45 *AI*, 1000; Clarke, 'Sitriuc Silkbeard', *DIB*, 8, p. 975. **46** *AU*, 1000. **47** *AI*, 1001; *AU*, 1001. **48** *AU*, 1001. **49** *AI*, 1002; *AU*, 1002. **50** *CGRG*, pp 118–19.

battle, should he refuse hostages'.[50] *CGRG* relates that Máelsechnaill 'requested a month's delay to muster *Leth Cuinn*', to which Brian agreed. It goes on to record that while Brian and his army camped at Tara, Máelsechnaill sent a poet to Áed Ua Néill (son of the previous high-king Domnall), the king of Cenél nEógain, and messengers to the other kings of *Leth Cuinn* to 'come unanimously … to give furious and manly battle to Brian and the *Leth Moga*, and to contend for the freedom of Tara with them'. Máelsechnaill is also reported to have added that, if help was not forthcoming, 'the counsel he adopted was to give hostages to Brian because he had not the power by himself to meet the *Leth Moga*'. This was a very sensible statement and it indicates that Máelsechnaill may simply not have been able to match the growing power of Brian as his kingdom of Munster grew wealthy and more capable and as Brian also added the forces of Dublin and Leinster to his army.

CGRG states that Máelsechnaill's poet composed a poem as he addressed Áed Ua Néill. It is quite long, but at one point urges Ua Néill:

> *Ar baig Goedel geib do sciath*
> *Co sin oenfer forges cach,*
> *Na leic tor Temra i tech mBriain,*
> *It[s]elba bai biaid co brath.*

> For the sake of the Gael take thy shield
> Against that one man who injures all;
> Let not the Hill of Tara come into Brian's house,
> With those who now possess it let it be forever.[51]

If factual, this poem was a strong appeal to the common Uí Néill sentiment of the Cenél nEógain, but Máelsechnaill's embassy failed. *CGRG* states that Áed Ua Néill replied: 'When … the Cenél nEógain had Tara, they defended its freedom; and whoever possesses it, let him defend its freedom'.

51 Ibid., pp 122–3.

Ua Néill is reputed to have added 'that he would not risk his life in battle against the Dál Cais, in defence of sovereignty for any other man'. *CGRG* relates that Máelsechnaill, when informed of Ua Néill's refusal to assist him, actually travelled north to Ua Néill's palace and offered him the hostages of the Southern Uí Néill, stating: 'Defend Tara for thyself and I will give thee hostages; for I would rather be dependent on thee than on Brian'. Áed Ua Néill then called a secret council of the nobles of Cenél nEógain that suggested that their king assist Máelsechnaill, but only if the king of Meath ceded half his kingdom to the Cenél nEógain 'as if it had been their inheritance'. *CGRG* concludes this piece by stating that the answer of the nobles of Cenél nEógain so infuriated King Máelsechnaill that he immediately proceeded to Tara and submitted to Brian 'without guarantee or protection, beyond the honour of Brian himself'.[52] Brian was now high-king of Ireland and a real king of all but the northern kingdoms of Ireland.

The reasons for the collapse of the Uí Néill high-kingship are not clear. Máelsechnaill II evidently could no longer match the growing power of King Brian. Máelsechnaill's main support in his fight against Brian in these years came from the king of Connacht. He needed the support of the Cenél nEógain, one of the greatest warrior dynasties on the island, if he was successfully to combat the king of Munster. There does not appear to have been any support forthcoming from the Cenél nEógain, even though this dynasty was also from the Uí Néill and the king of Cenél nEógain was expected to succeed Máelsechnaill as high-king. It is unclear why Áed Ua Néill, the king of Cenél nEógain, refused to support Máelsechnaill in 1002, or in the years beforehand. There may have been a personality clash between the two kings, but something appears to have happened in the kingdom of Meath during the high-kingship of Áed's father, Domnall Ua Néill. In their record of the year 971, AU record that 'Domnall Ua Néill, king of Tara, was driven from Meath by the Clann Cholmáin'. A few entries later, but under the same year, the same annals state that 'Domnall Ua Néill led an army against the men of Meath, and plundered all their churches and

52 Ibid., pp 120–31.   53 *AU*, 971; MacShamhráin, 'Brian Bóruma, Armagh and high kingship', 15.

forts'.[53] The Roll of the Kings, a medieval Irish text attached to the late eleventh-century Lebor Gabála Erenn, adds that afterwards 'Meath was desert [meaning there was no king] for five years till Máelsechlainn took it' (*Mide fás cóic bliadna corragaib Máelsechlainn mac Domnaill*).[54] What exactly happened in Meath this year is uncertain, but it appears to have been dramatic. It seems to have greatly soured relations between the Cenél nEógain and Clann Cholmáin and led to a grave weakening of the Uí Néill high-kingship. The two dynasties may simply have grown apart, however, over a number of centuries.[55]

BRIAN BECOMES KING OF ALL IRELAND

Brian appears to have been a king who was determined to be the effective ruler of the entire island of Ireland. He was not content to be high-king of the two southern thirds of Ireland, something that was still an immense achievement for a king of Munster. He could now put an extremely large army (by medieval Irish standards) into the field made up of the Munster army, large and capable in its own right, but now with added contingents from the kingdoms of Leinster, Connacht, Meath and Dublin. Of these additions, the soldiers of Meath and Dublin would have been the most valuable, Máelsechnaill's soldiers being very experienced and the men from Dublin well armed in Scandinavian fashion with coats of mail, shields, axes and swords. The Dubliners also provided the high-king with a substantial fleet of longships when required.

The king from Munster had now only to subdue the north of Ireland to become the effective high-king. There were three main kingdoms in the north, Cenél Conaill and Cenél nEógain of the Northern Uí Néill and the Ulaid kingdom east of Lough Neagh and the River Bann. Of these

---

54 Stewart MacAlister (ed.), *Lebor Gabála Erenn*, 5, pp 402–3; I am very grateful to my old tutor, Prof. Francis John Byrne, who once discussed this collapse of the Uí Néill high-kingship with me many years ago.   **55** See also F.J. Byrne, *The rise of the Uí Néill and the high-kingship of Ireland* (Dublin, 1969).

opponents, only the king of Cenél nEógain was a powerful adversary. The Cenél nEógain kingdom was large, stretching from the Inishowen Peninsula to south of Armagh. It also had a mountainous and forested interior. More importantly, the Cenél nEógain had a strong warrior tradition and their kings were, in their own right, used to being high-kings of Ireland. In contrast, Cenél Conaill, while also a warrior Uí Néill kingdom, was quite small and isolated and tended to follow the lead of the king of Cenél nEógain. Ulaid was a weak kingdom and its rulers were much more afraid of the king of Cenél nEógain than they were of a far-off high-king in Munster. In 1004 there was a big battle at Craeb Tulca in modern Co. Antrim when the Cenél nEógain, assisted by the Cenél Conaill, inflicted a very heavy defeat on the Ulaid. Eochaid, king of the Ulaid, and a large number of Ulaid nobles were killed. Áed Ua Néill, king of Cenél nEógain, was also killed in murky circumstances.[56] He was succeeded by his nephew Flaithbertach Ua Néill.

Brian had severe difficulty in forcing Flaithbertach to acknowledge him as king of Ireland. Ua Néill was a young leader compared to Brian Boru, being born in 977.[57] This was the same year in which Amlaíb Cuarán the Hiberno-Norse king of Dublin killed his father Muirchertach Midheach, who was the son of Domnall Ua Néill the high-king at the time.[58] Soon after becoming king in 1004 Flaithbertach and the Cenél nEógain 'prevented' Brian from making 'a circuit' of their territory.[59] Brian had to wait two years until 1006 before he succeeded in forcing 'an army on a circuit of Ireland' through Cenél Conaill, Cenél nEógain and Ulaid in a show of strength.[60] The next year Brian thwarted Flaithbertach's invasion of the kingdom of the Ulaid when Ua Néill 'took seven pledges' from them.[61] Brian marched into Cenél nEogáin and 'took the hostages of Ulaid from the king of Aileach by force'.[62] When Ua Néill raided into Brega in 1009 'and took a great tribute in cows', Brian had had enough.[63] In 1010, he led

56 *AU*, 1004; *AI*, 1004; Darren McGettigan and Ailbhe MacShamhráin, 'Áed Ua Néill', *DIB*, 9, p. 597. **57** *AU*, 977. **58** Ibid.; Hogan, 'The Irish law of kingship, with special reference to Ailech and Cenél Eoghain', pl. v. **59** *AU*, 1004. **60** Ibid., 1006; *AI*, 1006. **61** *AU*, 1007. **62** *AI*, 1007; *AU*, 1007. **63** *AU*, 1009.

'a great hosting of the men of Munster' as far as Armagh and Flaithbertach Ua Néill conceded defeat and 'gave Brian his demand in full and Brian brought Ua Néill's hostages to Kincora'.[64] It is probably at this time that Brian's daughter Bebhinn married Ua Néill, although, as will become apparent, this marriage alliance did not engender much loyalty on the part of Flaithbertach to his new father-in-law.[65]

Brian finished the job of becoming the monarch of the entire island when in 1011 he invaded Cenél Conaill twice in the one year. The first time he had with him 'a great muster of the men of Ireland'. His sons Murchad and Domnall each took half of the army and 'harried Cenél Conaill'.[66] Flaithbertach Ua Néill assisted Murchad in seizing '300 captives and many cows'.[67] When Brian returned later in the same year with 'a great hosting ... by land and sea', the king of Cenél Conaill, Máelruanaid Ua Máil Doraid, personally surrendered to Brian and accompanied the high-king to Kincora where he 'accepted a large stipend from him, and made complete submission to him'.[68] This conquest of Cenél Conaill by Brian Boru is one of the most thorough and accomplished invasions of an Irish kingdom by another Irish king recorded in the annals. It was probably the fleet brought to the north-west by Brian that ensured the success of his second expedition.

BRIAN AND ARMAGH

While campaigning against the Cenél nEogáin, Brian demonstrated how intelligent a king he was. In 1005, 'accompanied by the royalty of Ireland', he travelled to Armagh, the centre of Christianity on the island. Once in Armagh, Brian 'left twenty ounces of gold on Patrick's altar'.[69] Brian also recognized Armagh as the ecclesiastical capital of Ireland. By doing so, he demonstrated a shrewdness and strength of purpose not often shown by Irish kings. A less resolute or far-sighted king might have attempted to support a Munster monastery such as Emly (the Eóganacht dynasties did

64 *AI*, 1010; *AU*, 1010. 65 Ní Mhaonaigh, *Brian Boru*, p. 33. 66 *AI*, 1011. 67 *AU*, 1011. 68 *AI*, 1011; *AU*, 1011. 69 *AU*, 1005. 70 MacShamhráin, 'Brian Bóruma,

indeed try to promote Emly and the independence of the church in the south of Ireland).[70] Brian recognized the power already in Armagh's position and felt that it could enhance his own island-wide authority, even though Armagh was closely associated with the kings of Cenél nEogáin, Brian's most reluctant vassal. Indeed, it had been Muirecán, the coarb of Patrick, that had 'conferred kingly orders' on Áed Ua Néill in 993, after which Muirecán had been granted 'a visitation of Cenél nEógain ... [and] a great visitation of the north of Ireland'.[71] Máel Muire, the man who succeeded Muirecán as coarb of Patrick in 1001, appears to have viewed King Brian with favour.[72]

During the 1005 visit, the high-king's secretary, Máel Suthain, made a note in the Book of Armagh, stating that he had 'found it in the books of the Irish' that St Patrick had ordered that Armagh be his apostolic church.[73] Máel Suthain added that Brian agreed to this 'for all the kings of Maceria', thought to refer to the Great Plain of Munster (*Machaire Mór na Muman*) or the Plain of Cashel (*Machaire Chaisil*). This is the famous note where Máel Suthain described King Brian as 'Emperor of the Irish' (*Imperatoris Scotorum*).[74] The full entry reads:

> St Patrick, going up to heaven, commanded that all the fruit of his labour, as well as baptisms as of causes and of alms, should be carried to the apostolic city which is called in Irish Armagh. Thus I have found it in the books of the Irish. I, that is Máel Suthain, have written this in the sight of Brian, Emperor of the Irish; and what I have, he has determined for all the kings of Maceria.[75]

The following year, Brian granted Máel Muire, the coarb of Armagh, 'the full demand of the community of Patrick', by which time an agent for

Armagh and high kingship', 1.   **71** *AU*, 993.   **72** Ibid., 1001; Ailbhe MacShamhráin, 'Máel Muire', *DIB*, 6, p. 224.   **73** Aubrey Gwynn, 'Brian in Armagh (1005)', *Seanchas Ard Mhacha*, 9:1 (1978), 46; Aidan Breen, 'Máel Suthain', *DIB*, 6, pp 226–7.   **74** John Gwynn (ed.), *Liber Ardmachanus: The Book of Armagh* (Dublin, 1913), fo. 16v; *AFM*, 1031 (note 1).   **75** MacShamhráin, 'Brian Bóruma, Armagh and high kingship', 16.   **76** *AU*, 1006; *AFM*, 1006; MacShamhráin, 'Brian Bóruma, Armagh and high kingship', 1.

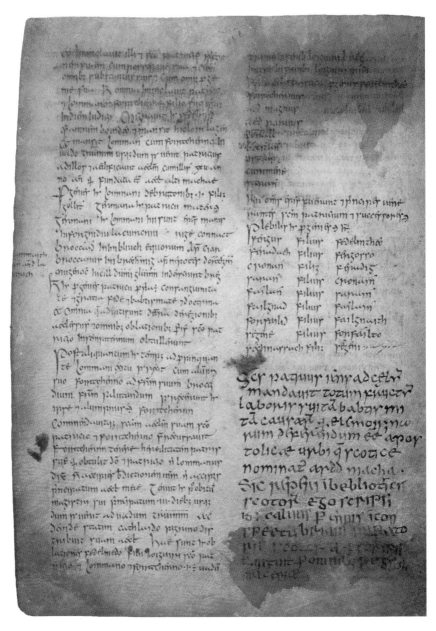

15 The famous 'Emperor of the Irish' note written into the Book of Armagh (TCD MS 52, fo. 16v) in 1005 by Brian Boru's secretary, Máel Suthain, as King Brian looked on (courtesy of the Board of Trinity College Dublin).

Armagh, 'Tuathal Ua Maoilmacha, a learned man and comharba of Patrick in Munster', was active in the southern kingdom.[76] Brian's use of the title 'Emperor of the Irish' is thought to have been in imitation of the German Emperor Otto III who died in January 1002, having 'received the imperial anointment' from his cousin Pope Gregory V in Rome in May 996.[77] Otto III was said to have been 'consecrated … august emperor, to the acclamation not only of the Romans, but of all the people of Europe'.[78] The medieval Irish were well informed about the German Empire through the continued links between the island and some of the monasteries founded in German towns by Irish missionaries in earlier centuries.

AT THE COURT OF BRIAN BORU

There is little evidence that Brian was the great reforming king of legend. It is likely that the author of *CGRG* largely invented his programmes for rebuilding churches and monasteries, laying down new roads and bridges, and commissioning copies of lost Irish books destroyed in the earlier Viking invasions of Ireland.[79] Brian did patronize the building of a few stone churches and round towers at ecclesiastical sites in the territory of the Dál Cais, as well as at a number of additional sites in the modern counties of Limerick and Tipperary.[80] A fragment of a shrine from the church at Leamakevoge in Co. Tipperary that reads '[Brian M]ac Cenedic, king of Ire[land]', preserves the high-king's association with this building.[81] The total number, however, is quite small. Nevertheless, Brian's reign as king of

77 Gwynn, 'Brian in Armagh (1005)', 44; MacShamhráin, 'Brian Bóruma, Armagh and high kingship', 17; David A. Warner (ed. and trans.), *Ottonian Germany: the Chronicon of Thietmar of Merseburg* (Manchester, 2001), 996, 1002, pp 170–1, 187; this idea was first suggested by Prof. Eoin MacNeill in 1919. **78** Warner (ed. and trans.), *The Chronicon of Thietmar of Merseburg*, p. 171 (note 87: 'The Annals of Quedlinburg'); Eliza Garrison, *Ottonian imperial art and portraiture: the artistic patronage of Otto III and Henry II* (Farnham, 2012). **79** *CGRG*, pp 136–41. **80** Tomás Ó Carragáin, *Churches in early medieval Ireland: architecture, ritual and memory* (London, 2010), pp 124–5, 131–2; Gwynn and Hadcock, *Medieval religious houses: Ireland*, pp 37, 40, 46, 96–7. **81** Ó Carragáin, *Churches in early medieval Ireland*, p. 133.

16 The Liathmore fragment: a small bronze strip, possibly part of an early eleventh-century shrine, discovered in a layer of clay on the floor of Leamakevoge Church during archaeological excavations undertaken in the 1940s. The fourteen complete letters and two partial ones laid in silver read ... AC CENEDIC DORIG ER ... (... [M]ac Cenedic, king of Ire[land]) and can only refer to Brian Boru (courtesy of the National Museum of Ireland).

Munster from 978 to 1014 was extremely peaceful by medieval Irish standards. This peace was gradually extended to the rest of Ireland, as his power grew as king of the whole island. Leinster was peaceful from 999 to 1013, while the kingdom of Meath enjoyed Brian's peace from the year 1002, when Máelsechnaill II abdicated the high-kingship, to 1012. These are exceptionally long periods in a medieval Irish context. It is these extended peaceful times throughout much of Ireland for almost forty years that probably gave rise to the later legends about Brian recounted in the twelfth-century Cogadh Gaedhel re Gallaibh. The most famous legend is the well-known statement that 'after the banishment of the foreigners out of all Erin, and after Erin was reduced to a state of peace, a lone woman came from Torach, in the north of Erin, to Cliodhna, in the south of Erin, carrying a ring of gold on a horse-rod, and she was neither robbed nor insulted'.[82] (The legend records that the woman travelled from Tory Island off the coast of Co. Donegal to the 'Wave of Clíona', a natural strong tide in Glandore Bay, West Cork.)[83]

Brian's court at Kincora does appear to have been a cultured and remarkable place. The high-king's palace became famous, not only in Ireland but also in the Scandinavian world, where it was known as Kankaraborg.[84] As king, Brian surrounded himself with learned people such as his secretary Máel Suthain (d. 1031), who is recorded elsewhere as his *anmchara* (modern

---

82 *CGRG*, pp 138–9.   **83** Dáithí Ó hÓgáin, *Myth, legend and romance: an encyclopaedia of the Irish folk tradition* (London, 1990), pp 90–2.   **84** Albertus Johannes Goedheer, *Irish and Norse traditions about the Battle of Clontarf* (Haarlem, 1938), p. 92.

17 (*opposite*) A panel from the eleventh-century shrine of St Maelruain's Missal, showing two clerics and a harper (the fourth figure is an angel), which may represent a scene from the court of King Brian or his son Donnchadh (courtesy of the National Museum of Ireland).

Irish *anam cara*) or spiritual advisor.[85] The court of Brian's great rival, King Máelsechnaill II, was also a very cultured place. The famous poet Giollachomhghaill Ua Slebhene, attached to his court (d. 1031), was the man reputed to have brought the request for assistance to the palace of King Áed Ua Néill of Cenél nEógain in 1002.[86] Guesting and feasting, which remained an important part of Irish culture for centuries to come, were prominent in the social life of Kincora. Brian's drinking horn was preserved by the Dál Cais until the year 1151, when it was given away by one of his descendants in a moment of crisis.[87] At court, Brian's sons Murchad, Domnall (d. 1011), Donnchadh and Tadhg played important roles.[88] I doubt, however, the prominent parts given to his queen Gormlaith and her brother Máelmórda, king of Leinster, as recounted in the sagas during the build-up to the Battle of Clontarf.[89] Máelmórda strikes me as a minor figure, little more than a thoroughly subjugated vassal of his nephew King Sitric Silkenbeard of Dublin.

BRIEFLY KING OF THE ENTIRE ISLAND

For a brief few months in 1011–12, Brian Boru was effective high-king of the entire island of Ireland. This was an astounding achievement, especially for a king from Munster. It was even more so for a man of such obscure dynastic origins. The success of the Dál Cais was solely due to the talent, ambition and determination of Brian's immediate family. Now that he was king of Ireland, Brian needed to be aware of the potential threats to his all-powerful position. He knew that he had to be wary of Sitric Silkenbeard.

85 *AFM*, 1031; John O'Donohue, *Anam Cara: spiritual wisdom from the Celtic world* (London, 1997). **86** *CGRG*, pp 120–7. **87** *AFM*, 1151. **88** *AI*, 1011. **89** *CGRG*, pp 142–7.

Sitric had already led one major rebellion against his father-in-law, and although in 999 the Dublin army had been ruthlessly crushed at the Battle of Glenn Máma, Brian knew what a potentially dangerous adversary the Hiberno-Norse king could be. Although the Dublin men were quiet and seemingly loyal to Brian after 999, serving in his army and providing ships for his fleets, the neighbouring Anglo-Saxon kingdom of England came under severe attack in the early eleventh century. Large Viking fleets and armies led by such powerful figures as Svein Forkbeard, king of Denmark, and his son Cnut raided throughout England. If Brian was aware of these attacks, he may have feared Sitric of Dublin being noticed by someone like Svein Forkbeard and possibly attracting a large Viking force to Dublin. Indeed, there were enough powerful Viking freelance raiders in England at this time for this to be a definite possibility. King Svein conquered the entire kingdom of England in 1013 after expelling the Anglo-Saxon ruler, Æthelred the *Unraed*.[90] Svein Forkbeard died on 2 or 3 February 1014, before he could show any interest in the kingdom of Dublin.[91] In the end, when he did rebel, Sitric Silkenbeard had to look much further north than to the Danish invaders of Anglo-Saxon England for assistance.

A revolt of the Uí Néill was probably considered the most likely possibility. Proud dynasties such as the Clann Cholmáin and Cenél nEógain would naturally be waiting for a favourable opportunity to rebel against Brian and seize the high-kingship again. Despite this, Máelsechnaill II appears to have been content to be loyal to Brian as high-king in the years after 1002. Brian considered the king of Meath to be a valued and reliable vassal. Also in 1004, Máelsechnaill II 'fell [from his horse] so that he lay mortally ill'.[92] (According to later legend, Máelsechnaill was an excellent horseman and had a passion for breaking in untrained horses.)[93] This accident seems to have had a severe effect on Máelsechnaill and he was not so able in the years after his fall as he was in his prime. Brian certainly needed to watch his second son-in-law, Flaithbertach Ua Néill, the king of Cenél nEogáin. It had taken a great deal of trouble to force Ua Néill to

90 *ASC*, 1013. **91** Ibid., 1014; Ryan Lavelle, *Aethelred II: king of the English, 978–1016* (Stroud, 2002), p. 130. **92** *AU*, 1004. **93** *AFM*, 989 [recte 990] (note t).

submit in 1010 and Flaithbertach was still active as a raiding king. In 1011, Ua Néill burned down an Ulaid fortress on the banks of the River Lagan, which belonged to the king of Dál Fiatach.[94] For whatever reason, Brian does not appear to have regarded this as a hostile act. The high-king, however, was able to detach Máelruanaid Ua Máil Doraid, the king of Cenél Conaill, from the Cenél nEogáin by creating a strong personal link with him as a valued vassal.

94 *AU*, 1011.

3 Viking warriors:
'The foreigners of the armour'

The year 980 was also the year that Viking raiders began their great attack on the Anglo-Saxon kingdom of England in what has become known to historians as the 'Second Viking Age'.[1] In that year, the Anglo-Saxon Chronicles record that 'Southampton was ravaged by a raiding-army and most of the town-dwellers killed or taken prisoner. And the same year the land of Thanet was raided; and the same year Cheshire was raided by a northern raiding ship-army'.[2] By the 990s, the Viking raiders had invaded East Anglia and began to demand immense 'taxes' from the English to be bought off, although the raiders always returned.[3] In 991 the Norwegian Viking leader Olaf Tryggvason won a major victory over the Anglo-Saxons when the army of Ealdorman Byrhtnoth was defeated with heavy losses at the Battle of Maldon, fought on the coast of Essex (10 or 11 August 991).[4] In 994, Svein Forkbeard, in the company of Olaf Tryggvason, laid siege to the town of London until they were paid £16,000 by the Anglo-Saxons to leave.[5] The raids became more extensive in the years 997 to 1002, with more tribute paid and much damage done to the Anglo-Saxon kingdom. In 1002, the English king, Æthelred the *Unraed* (this king's nickname was a clever Anglo-Saxon pun as the full name literally meant 'good advice the ill-advised'),[6] after first paying off the Scandinavians with £24,000, 'in the middle of this ordered all the Danish men who were among the English race to be killed on Brice's Day, because it was made known to the king that they wanted to ensnare his life – and afterwards all his councillors – and

1 Forte, Oram and Pedersen (eds), *Viking empires*, pp 184–216. 2 *ASC*, 980.
3 £10,000 was paid in 991; *ASC*, 991. 4 Ibid., 991; James Campbell (ed.), *The Anglo-Saxons* (London, 1982), pp 173, 195, 198; Lavelle, *Aethelred II*, pp 68–71; S.A.J. Bradley (ed.), *Anglo-Saxon poetry* (London, 1982), pp 518–28. 5 *ASC*, 994. 6 Lavelle, *Aethelred II*, pp 7–10; Campbell (ed.), *The Anglo-Saxons*, p. 193

have his kingdom afterwards'.[7] Evidence exists that the Anglo-Saxon king's orders were at least carried out at Oxford and one of the most prominent Danish casualties may have been King Svein Forkbeard's sister.[8] Forkbeard returned to raid in England in 1003–5. In 1006, the Viking army 'travelled just where it wanted, and the campaign caused the local people every kind of harm'.[9] In 1009, the independent Viking leader Thorkell the Tall invaded eastern England with his 'immense hostile raiding army', composed of Danes, Swedes and Norwegians.[10] Thorkell extracted many 'taxes' from the Anglo-Saxons, totalling £48,000, and in 1012 his warriors captured the ecclesiastical city of Canterbury, where Archbishop Ælfheah was killed by some 'very drunk' Vikings, who were 'much stirred up against the bishop, because he did not want to offer them any money'.[11] Svein Forkbeard returned to England in 1013 when Thorkell the Tall joined King Æthelred and the English. Svein drove Æthelred into exile and 'the whole nation' of England had Svein 'as full king'.[12]

These events, which convulsed the Anglo-Saxon kingdom of England, must have been known in Ireland. They were certainly known to the Hiberno-Norse in Dublin. During these eventful years in England, Sitric Silkenbeard became king of Dublin in 989 and the St Brice's Day massacre (13 November 1002) took place in the year that Máelsechnaill II surrendered the high-kingship of Ireland to Brian.[13] The Vikings were on the march in England in the first years of the eleventh century and their astounding success must have alarmed the major Irish kings. After 1002, King Brian had to protect the southern two-thirds of Ireland as high-king and overlord, while at the same time he attempted to reduce the north of the island to vassal status. Brian's worst fear might have been the arrival in Ireland of Viking forces under an independent leader such as Thorkell the Tall, and their seizure of one of the Hiberno-Norse towns such as Waterford or Dublin. From such a base, a Scandinavian raiding army could easily have set out into the Irish interior to challenge Brian's high-kingship. The danger

---

7 *ASC*, 1002. 8 Lavelle, *Aethelred II*, pp 99–104. 9 *ASC*, 1006. 10 Ibid., 1009; Forte, Oram and Pedersen (eds), *Viking empires*, pp 190–1. 11 *ASC*, 1012. 12 Ibid., 1013.

of this occurring may actually have been very real. According to the Icelandic sagas, Olaf Tryggvason married Amlaíb Cuarán's sister Gytha and was familiar with Ireland, having 'harried far and wide' there in his younger days.[14] The Welsh Chronicle of the Princes also records that during the 994–5 campaign season Svein Forkbeard 'ravaged Man', which must have been uncomfortably west for the major Irish kings.[15]

Sitric Silkenbeard, the Hiberno-Norse king of Dublin, was an influential figure in the western Scandinavian world at this time. He appears as a recurring character in many of the thirteenth-century Icelandic sagas. This includes a prominent appearance in Gunnlaugs Saga, written about the adventures of a young Icelandic skald (Old Norse/Icelandic *skáld*: an Icelander who became a specialist in court poetry) called Gunnlaugr *ormstunga* (serpent-tongue).[16] Some time in the years 1003 or 1004, Gunnlaugr is reputed to have visited the court of Sitric Silkenbeard at Dublin.[17] According to the saga, Gunnlaugr made his way to Dublin 'with some merchants northwards from England'. Sitric 'gave him a fitting welcome',[18] but 'never before honoured by a skald, has to be dissuaded from rewarding Gunnlaugr for his … poem with the amusingly inflated gift of two ships. Instead, Gunnlaugr receives a set of the king's clothes and an arm-ring worth one mark'.[19] As the saga put it:

> The king thanked him for the poem and called his treasurer to him and said 'How should I reward the poem?' 'How do you wish, lord?', he replied. 'How would it be rewarded', asked the king, 'if I gave him a couple of merchant ships?' 'That's too much, my lord', answered the treasurer. 'As rewards for poems, other kings give

13 *AU*, 989. 14 McGettigan, 'Amlaíb (Óláfr) Cuarán', *DIB*, 1, p. 98; Lee M. Hollander (ed.), *Heimskringla: history of the kings of Norway* (Austin, TX, 1964), pp 169–73; Bo Almqvist and Dáithí Ó hÓgáin, *Skálda: Éigse is eachtraíocht sa tsean-lochlainn* (Baile Átha Cliath, 1995), p. 28. 15 *Brut Y Tywysogyon*, 994–5, p. 10. 16 Russell Poole (ed.), *Skaldsagas: text, vocation, and desire in the Icelandic sagas of poets* (Berlin, 2000), p. 1. 17 P.G. Foote (ed.) and R. Quirk (trans.), *The Saga of Gunnlaug Serpent-Tongue* (London, 1957), pp xxii–xxiv. 18 Ibid., p. 18. 19 Diana Whaley, 'Representations of skalds in the sagas 1: social and professional relations' in Poole (ed.), *Skaldsagas*, pp 290–1.

valuable treasures, fine swords or gold bracelets'. The king gave him his own clothes made of new and precious cloth, an embroidered tunic, a cloak lined with precious furs and a gold bracelet weighing half a pound. Gunnlaugr thanked him gracefully and stayed there a short time. He went from there to the Orkneys.[20]

Sitric's importance in the Scandinavian world can be gauged by the fact that when Gunnlaugr visited Jarl Sigurd Hlodvisson in Orkney next, a less prestigious type of poetry was used to praise the ruler of the northern islands. Gunnlaugr *ormstunga* ended this part of his travels at the court of King Olaf the Swede in Sweden.

Olaf Tryggvason and King Svein invaded England in 994 with '4-and-ninety ships', while Thorkell the Tall joined King Æthelred in 1012 with '45 ships from the raiding-army'.[21] King Svein probably commanded many thousands of well-armed Viking warriors.[22] The fleet of 994 is estimated to have 'carried a force of more than two thousand fighting men'.[23] One can only imagine the damage a large royal Scandinavian army would have done in Ireland at this period, even if opposed by King Brian's elite Munster soldiers. To Brian, an invasion by someone such as Svein Forkbeard would have been a disaster. The Anglo-Saxons of England, who had quite a good army themselves, proved incapable of successfully meeting the Viking warriors of this second age in battle.[24] The drastic decline in Anglo-Saxon military prowess around the year AD1000 owed much to the lack of prestiege of Æthelred's kingship caused by the murder of his brother King Edward in 978.[25] This murder, which led to Æthelred's succession, also caused a collapse in 'the instinctive loyalty of the common people' to the Anglo-Saxon monarchy and may even have prompted the Scandinavians to launch their attacks on England.[26]

20 Foote (ed.), *The Saga of Gunnlaug Serpent-Tongue*, pp 18–19. **21** *ASC*, 994, 1012. **22** Niels Lund, 'The armies of Swein Forkbeard and Cnut: *leding* or *lið*?', *Anglo-Saxon England*, 15 (1986), 105–18. **23** Frank Stenton, *Anglo-Saxon England* (Oxford, 1971/2001), p. 378. **24** Lawson, *Cnut: England's Viking king*, pp 125–72. **25** *ASC*, 978. **26** Stenton, *Anglo-Saxon England*, pp 373–4; Dorothy Whitelock (ed.), *Sermo Lupi Ad Anglos* (Exeter, 1976).

HARALD HARDRADI

Probably the greatest Viking warrior of this age was Harald Hardradi (Harald the Ruthless), who was king of Norway from 1047 until his death at the Battle of Stamford Bridge in England on 25 September 1066.[27] Harald Hardradi is famous as the commander of the Varangian guard (*Væringjar*) in the Byzantine Empire from the mid 1030s to 1042. Harald served the Empress Zoe in Sicily (where he fought under the Byzantine general George Maniakes, who was killed in 1043) and also in Bulgaria and his longships saw action against Muslim pirates in the Aegean.[28] Snorri Sturluson's saga, Heimskringla (history of the kings of Norway), portrays King Harald as a great example of a formidable Viking warrior. According to the saga, 'as soon as Harald reached Constantinople he presented himself to the empress and immediately joined her army as a mercenary … Soon after Harald joined the army, all the Varangians became very attached to him, and they fought side by side in battle. Eventually, Harald became the acknowledged leader of all the Varangians'.[29] The saga continues:

> whenever the whole army was engaged, Harald saw to it that his own men were kept out of the battle or else were stationed where the danger was least: he claimed that he was anxious to avoid losses among his men. But whenever he and his men were engaged on their own, he drove them into battle so fiercely that they either had to be victorious or be killed.[30]

According to Sturluson, Harald was also an extremely successful Scandinavian leader in the manner by which he 'amassed a vast hoard of wealth', which he sent 'by his own reliable messengers to Novgorod', to be kept in safety for him by his friend Jaroslav, prince of Kiev.[31] When Harald

---

27 Magnus Magnusson and Hermann Pálsson (eds), *Snorri Sturluson: King Harald's Saga* (London, 2005), pp 9–11. **28** Alexander P. Kazhdan (ed.), *The Oxford dictionary of Byzantium*, 2 (Oxford, 1991), pp 902, 1285; 3, p. 2228. **29** *King Harald's Saga*, p. 48. **30** Ibid., p. 50. **31** Ibid., p. 52.

Hardradi left Byzantine service, Prince Jaroslav handed over the treasure at Novgorod, by which time 'this hoard of wealth was so immense that no one in northern Europe had ever seen the like of it in one man's possession'.[32] Verses of Scandinavian poetry preserved in the saga describe Harald as a great warrior. One verse composed by the Icelander Thjodolf Arnorsson, who was court poet to King Magnus the Good, states:

> All men know that Harald
> Fought eighteen savage battles;
> Wherever the warrior went
> All hope of peace was shattered.
> The grey eagle's talons
> You reddened with blood, great king;
> On all your expeditions
> The hungry wolves were feasted.[33]

Harald eventually fell out with the Byzantines owing to his fondness for the custom of 'palace-plunder'. Sturluson's saga states that 'it is the custom there that every time an emperor dies, the Varangians are allowed palace-plunder – they are entitled to ransack all the palaces where the emperor's treasures are kept and to take freely whatever each can lay his hands on'.[34] Sturluson recorded that Harald 'had three times taken part in a palace-plunder'. In the winter of 1042–3, Harald Hardradi escaped and returned to Kiev for his treasure and his new bride, Elizabeth, the daughter of Prince Jaroslav.[35] Harald became king of Norway in 1047 and when he invaded the north of the kingdom of England in 1066 he had with him an estimated force of 200–300 longships and a huge army estimated at the time at nine-thousand men.[36]

32 Ibid., p. 64. **33** Ibid., pp 58–9. **34** Ibid., p. 64. **35** *Oxford dictionary of Byzantium*, 2, p. 902. **36** *King Harald's Saga*, p. 10; *ASC*, 1066.

THE JARLS OF ORKNEY

Harald Hardradi was the greatest Viking warrior of the first half of the eleventh century. Closer to Ireland and actually involved in the Battle of Clontarf was Sigurd Hlodvisson the Stout, jarl of Orkney, an island realm that covered most of the islands to the north and west of Scotland, and some of the northern Scottish mainland as well. The islands of Orkney and Shetland, which were fertile and fully colonized by Scandinavians, had a large population at the beginning of the eleventh century.[37] Caithness and Sutherland on the Scottish mainland were also heavily settled in their coastal parts. In the *Sudreyjar*, the islands now known as the Hebrides, the islands of Skye, Islay and Colonsay retain evidence of heavy Scandinavian settlement, while the large island of Lewis seems also to have been colonized by the Vikings to a substantial extent.[38] The Hebrides were never as fully Scandinavian as Orkney and Shetland. According to one early twentieth-century expert, 'the men of those parts appear to have regarded the Hebrideans, if not as strangers, at least not as real countrymen'.[39] The Orcadians spoke a dialect of Old Norse, later called Norn, throughout the medieval period.

The Icelandic sagas state that the jarldom of Orkney was first created by the famous founder of the kingdom of Norway, King Harald Fine-Hair (*c*.AD860–*c*.940).[40] According to Orkneyinga Saga, King Harald 'one summer … sailed west over the North Sea in order to teach a lesson to certain Vikings whose plundering he could no longer tolerate. These Vikings used to raid in Norway over summer and had Shetland and Orkney as their winter base'.[41] Having dealt with the troublesome pirates, the story goes that King Harald granted the Orkney and Shetland islands to the prominent Norwegian nobleman, Jarl Rognvald of Møre. According

37 Ian G. Scott and Anna Ritchie, *Pictish and Viking-age carvings from Shetland* (Edinburgh, 2009), pp vii, 8–9.   **38** Peter Sawyer (ed.), *The Oxford illustrated history of the Vikings* (Oxford, 1997), pp 90–1; Reidar Th. Christiansen, *The Vikings and the Viking wars in Irish and Gaelic tradition* (Oslo, 1931), p. 4.   **39** Christiansen, *The Vikings and the Viking wars in Irish and Gaelic tradition*, pp 4–5.   **40** Forte, Oram and Pedersen (eds), *Viking empires*, pp 265–70.   **41** *Orkneyinga Saga*, p. 26.

to Orkneyinga Saga, Rognvald initially made two failed attempts to install family members in his new holdings. Eventually, the sagas say, Rognvald of Møre succeeded in setting up his youngest son Einar as jarl of the islands, from whom all the later jarls of Orkney were descended.[42] Einar's son, Jarl Thorfinn Skull-Splitter, was noted as 'a strong ruler and warrior'.[43] Thorfinn Skull-Splitter was the grandfather of Jarl Sigurd, who fought at Clontarf. Sigurd's father, Jarl Hlodvir, was said to have 'ruled well'.[44] Sigurd's mother was the Leinster woman, Eithne.[45] Orkneyinga Saga calls her 'the daughter of King Kjarval of Ireland', by which the saga-writer must mean one of the daughters of the famous king of Osraige, Cerball mac Dúnlainge, who became well known in Iceland for marrying his daughters to Scandinavian noblemen in the late ninth century. Cerball was known as *Kjarvalr Írakonungr* (Kjarvalr the Irish king) in the Scandinavian world.[46] King Cerball died in 888 and, given the passage of years, it is impossible that Eithne was his daughter. Perhaps she was his granddaughter or even a great-granddaughter.

The jarldom of Orkney is first recorded in reliable historical sources in the year 1014. Archaeological evidence, however, suggests that there were indeed earlier jarls before Sigurd Hlodvisson the Stout.[47] Sigurd became jarl of Orkney around AD985 and he is correctly described by the saga-writers as 'a powerful man and a great warrior'.[48] The Icelandic sagas relate that Sigurd reduced much of the *Sudreyjar* to vassal status when he bested local Scandinavian leaders and also extended his power into northern mainland Scotland (the Caithness region) by driving out the Scots.[49] Most of the *Sudreyjar* at this period appears to have been ruled by minor Scandinavian chieftains, known as the 'Lawmen of the Isles' (from Old Norse *lǫgmenn*, which was borrowed into Irish as *lagmainn*).[50] AFM record Viking raids on

---

42 Ibid., pp 26–32.   **43** Ibid., p. 33.   **44** Ibid., p. 36.   **45** Forte, Oram and Pedersen (eds), *Viking empires*, p. 271.   **46** *Orkneyinga Saga*, pp 36–7; Byrne, *Irish kings and high-kings*, p. 162.   **47** Alex Woolf, *From Pictland to Alba, 789–1070* (Edinburgh, 2007), pp 300–8; John Marsden, *Kings, mormaers, rebels: early Scotland's other royal family* (Edinburgh, 2010), pp 83–4.   **48** *Heimskringla*, pp 350–1.   **49** Forte, Oram and Pedersen (eds), *Viking empires*, pp 270–1; *Njal's Saga*, pp 139–40.   **50** Downham, *Viking kings of Britain and Ireland*, pp 49, 185.

Ireland, led by *na Ladgmainn* and *Lagmannaibh na ninnsedh*, in the years 960 and 974.[51] Amlaíb son of Lagmann, who accompanied Sigurd to Clontarf in 1014, may have been a later example of one of these chieftains.[52] According to Njal's Saga, Sigurd's tribute in the *Sudreyjar* was collected for him by a Hebridean jarl called Gilli. Njal's Saga adds that Gilli was tied very closely to the jarl of Orkney, since he 'was married to Sigurd's sister Hvarflod'.[53] As most of the 'lawmen' chieftains probably governed only individual islands, Sigurd may have appointed Gilli to be his deputy in the *Sudreyjar* to solve the problem of collecting tribute from a multitude of widely dispersed noblemen.

Njal's Saga also records the memory of fighting between some of the jarl of Orkney's adherents and a more formidable opponent, Gofraid king of *Innsi Gall*, 'king of the islands of the foreigners', whose base was in the southern Hebrides. King Gofraid died in 989.[54] Njal's Saga maintains that Sigurd 'owned' the territories of Ross, Moray, Sutherland and Argyll on the Scottish mainland.[55] Barring Sutherland, which was indeed a part of the jarldom of Orkney at this time, the claims made in the saga are probably greatly exaggerated. Sigurd may well have raided and levied tribute in all of the territories named at one time or another, but he could never have held such vast areas on the mainland against the Scots. Jarl Sigurd is also stated to have extended his power deep into the Irish Sea region, possibly raiding the island monastery of Iona in 986.[56] Orkneyinga Saga notes this aspect of the growth in the power of the jarl of Orkney, stating that he 'used to go on Viking expeditions every summer as well, plundering in the Hebrides, Scotland and Ireland'.[57]

The sagas add that Sigurd was forced to become a Christian in 995 by Olaf Tryggvason, who soon after became king of Norway. According to Heimskringla, Olaf 'took Jarl Sigurd prisoner on the island of Ronaldsay. … King Olaf then offered the jarl as a ransom to be baptized and adopt the true faith, to swear allegiance to him, and to proclaim Christianity in all the

51 *AFM*, 960, 972 [*recte* 974]; Woolf, *From Pictland to Alba*, pp 298, 300.   **52** *AU*, 1014.   **53** *Njal's Saga*, pp 138, 296.   **54** Ibid., pp 139–40, 152–3; *AU*, 989.   **55** *Njal's Saga*, p. 139.   **56** Ibid., pp 269–71; *AU*, 986.   **57** *Orkneyinga Saga*, p. 36.

Orkney Islands'.[58] Olaf is reputed to have added that 'he would devastate the islands with fire and flame, and lay the land waste unless the people accepted baptism'. According to the same saga, Sigurd, 'seeing the pinch he was in ... chose to be baptized. Then he and all those with him were Christened. Thereupon, the jarl swore allegiance to the king, giving him his son as hostage'.[59] By the time of the Battle of Clontarf, however, Sigurd and his men were Christian in name only.

After the death of King Olaf in the Battle of Svöld (fought in AD1000), the sagas state that Jarl Sigurd switched allegiance to the king of Alba (now Scotland), probably Mael Coluim son of Cinaed, when he married the king's daughter. He may have done this in a successful effort to cement his hold over his territories on the Scottish mainland.[60] There is no contemporary evidence that Brian Boru ever managed to exert any over-lordship over or exact any tribute from Gaelic Scotland as *CGRG* and some modern historians suggest.[61] King Mael Coluim, who ruled Alba from 1005 to 1034, was a powerful and expansionary ruler, who conquered the British kingdom of Strathclyde and the Anglo-Saxon province of Lothian and annexed them to his newly created kingdom of Scotland. Brian would have encountered major opposition had he attempted to encroach upon Mael Coluim's sphere of influence. There are no entries in any of the Irish annals that record Brian taking a fleet to Scotland and campaigning in that country. He only managed to subjugate the entire island of Ireland by the year 1011 and this effort was sufficiently difficult and intense to ensure that he had little time and few resources to spare for any designs on Gaelic Scotland.

AU record that one Scottish Gaelic nobleman, Domnall son of Eimen son of Cainnech '*mormaer* (possibly a Pictish word meaning 'sea steward') of Mar in Alba', fought in Brian's army at Clontarf.[62] This man may have been an exile from Scotland who Brian took into his service. Mar lay to the

58 *Heimskringla*, pp 351–2. **59** Ibid., p. 189. **60** Forte, Oram and Pedersen (eds), *Viking empires*, p. 271; Woolf, *From Pictland to Alba*, pp 225–48, 342–3; Marsden, *Kings, mormaers, rebels*, pp 90–8. **61** *CGRG*, pp 136–7; Seán Duffy, 'Ireland and Scotland, 1014–1169: contacts and caveats' in Smyth (ed.), *Seanchas*, p. 354. **62** *AU*, 1014.

north of the kingdom of Alba in the region of Moray that had its own ruling dynasty opposed to the kings of Scotland. Mael Coluim son of Cinaed is believed to have imposed his overlordship over Moray and Mar, and Domnall son of Eimen the *mormaer* of Mar may have been expelled from Scotland during this process. As King Mael Coluim was an ally of Sigurd Hlodvisson, the jarl of Orkney, the two may even have shared a Leinster connection. This king of Alba is described in the late eleventh- or early twelfth-century Irish poem Prophecy of Berchán as 'Son of a Leinster woman – *Mac mná Laighen*', possibly from the Liffey region in north Leinster.[63] These references in the prophecy suggest that Domnall son of Eimen was an exile from Scotland since King Mael Coluim would hardly have allowed a controlled nobleman travel to Ireland to oppose his own ally and maternal kinsmen.[64] AT record a precedent for Domnall son of Eimen's presence in Ireland in 1014. These annals state that three Scottish noblemen, *Mormaer* Cellach son of Findguine, *Mormaer* Cellach son of Bairid and *Mormaer* Donnchad son of Morgand, all of whom are thought to have possibly been from the Moray region, were in the service of the king of Cenél Conaill in 974.[65]

The Orkney Vikings were 'often simultaneously marauding sea-kings and hard working farmers'.[66] Orkneyinga Saga describes the life of one of the greatest Vikings from Orkney, the twelfth-century nobleman, Svein Asleifarson, who was from the small island of Gairsay. The saga states:

> This is how Svein used to live. Winter he would spend at home on Gairsay, where he entertained some eighty men at his own expense. His drinking hall was so big, there was nothing in Orkney to compare with it. In the spring, he had more than enough to occupy him, with a great deal of seed to sow, which he saw to carefully himself. Then when that job was done, he would go off plundering

---

63 Benjamin Hudson, *Prophecy of Berchán: Irish and Scottish high-kings of the early middle ages* (Westport, CT, 1996), pp 52, 90, 219–23; Woolf, *From Pictland to Alba*, p. 225. **64** Duffy, 'Ireland and Scotland, 1014–1169: contacts and caveats', pp 353–4. **65** *AT*, ii, pp 338–9; *AFM*, 974. **66** *Orkneyinga Saga*, p. 14.

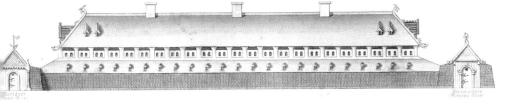

18 Drawing of a late Viking Age Icelandic nobleman's hall (exterior view), from Webbe Dasent (ed.), *The story of burnt Njal* (Edinburgh, 1861).

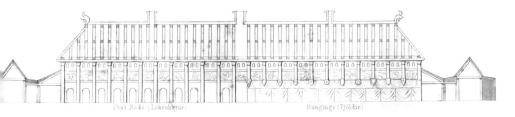

19 Drawing of a late Viking Age Icelandic nobleman's hall (interior view), from Webbe Dasent (ed.), *The story of burnt Njal* (Edinburgh, 1861).

in the Hebrides and in Ireland on what he called his 'spring trip', then back home just after midsummer, where he stayed till the cornfields had been reaped and the grain was safely in. After that he went off raiding again, and never came back till the first month of winter was ended. This he used call his 'autumn trip'.[67]

Jarl Sigurd's lifestyle in the Orkneys was no doubt little different from that of Svein Asleifarson. The jarls of Orkney could collect sizeable numbers of longships when the occasion required. At the sea battle of Roberry fought in the 1040s, Sigurd's son Thorfinn was able to gather 'sixty ships, most of them quite small' to fight for him, although his own longship was 'a big ship, well fitted out'. Jarl Thorfinn's adversary in the battle, his nephew Rognvald, 'had thirty large ships', but his force contained a major Norwegian element.[68] The size of these fleets may be approximately compared to that brought to Dublin by Sigurd in 1014. Sigurd's capital was

67 Ibid., pp 14, 215. **68** Ibid., pp 65–7.

20 The foundations of some eleventh-century Norse houses preserved at Birsay in the Orkneys, the capital of Jarl Sigurd the Stout (courtesy of Historic Scotland/Alba Aosmhor).

at Birsay, a small but easily defended tidal island in the Orkneys just off the coast of the largest island in the archipelago.[69]

THE ISLE OF MAN

The Isle of Man was an important centre of Scandinavian settlement in the Irish Sea. The island was very fertile and strategically located. Archaeological remains of pagan burials indicate that the first Vikings conquered the island in the late ninth and early tenth centuries. The substantial Viking warrior elite that settled came to rule over a larger pre-existing Celtic population.[70] The Scandinavians who colonized the Isle of

69 Forte, Oram and Pedersen (eds), *Viking empires*, pp 303–4.   **70** David Wilson, *The Vikings in the Isle of Man* (Gylling, 2008), pp 15–56; R. Andrew McDonald, *Manx*

Man became Christian within a generation or two. The large number of tenth-century decorated stone crosses on the island, which often have runic inscriptions, indicate that the settlers spoke 'Old West Norse'.[71] By the early eleventh century, the island's inhabitants of Viking descent had become quite wealthy, owing to extensive trade with Dublin and the Scandinavian markets to the north.[72] Although there are no references to Scandinavian kings of Man until the year 1070, the existence of a Dublin-influenced royal mint on the island, which began to produce coins from around the year 1025 onwards, suggests that there may have been earlier Manx kings of Hiberno-Norse origin.[73] The Viking rulers known as *rí Innsi Gall*, 'king of the islands of the foreigners' (probably the southern Hebrides), may also have had some power over the Isle of Man in the early eleventh century. Deaths of kings of *Innsi Gall* are noted in 989 and 1005.[74] AU record a large battle on the island in 987, which involved Scandinavian warriors and in which 'a thousand were slain'.[75] Brodir, the prominent noble who fought at Clontarf and who was associated with the Isle of Man, appears to have been the son of a Viking jarl called Audgisl, who came from York.[76] The political situation on Man in the years before 1014 was probably confused. Whatever authority the Scandinavian Manx kings or the kings of *Innsi Gall* may have possessed was possibly quite weak. Brodir may have utilized any confusion on the island at this time to conquer part of the Isle of Man. Alternatively, he may have had permission to settle on Man from a Manx king or a king of *Innsi Gall*.

These, therefore, were the type of Viking warrior that King Brian had to face on the battlefield of Clontarf in 1014. When Sitric Silkenbeard of Dublin rebelled against Brian in 1013, he may have intended to appeal for support to Svein Forkbeard of Denmark, who became king of England that year. Svein, however, died on 2 or 3 February 1014 and the return of the Anglo-Saxon king Æthelred the *Unraed* forced Svein's heir Cnut to retreat

kingship in its Irish Sea setting, 1187–1229: King Rognvaldr and the Crovan dynasty (Dublin, 2007), pp 42–3.　**71** Wilson, *The Vikings in the Isle of Man*, pp 57–86.　**72** Ibid., pp 105–18.　**73** Ibid., pp 115–16, 119–22.　**74** *AU*, 989, 1005.　**75** Ibid., 987.　**76** Ailbhe MacShamhráin, 'Brodir', *DIB*, 1, p. 849.

to Denmark. As a result, Scandinavian power in England was temporarily at a low-ebb in the early months of 1014. Cnut did not return to England with a large army until 1015.[77] If this was the case, King Sitric, undaunted, travelled north to the Viking rulers of Man and Orkney. He was not to be disappointed in his appeals for help against Brian. Sitric may even have found Sigurd of Orkney at a good time, with the jarl possibly impressed by Svein's exploits in England and planning to emulate the Dane by conquering land in Ireland. If victorious at Clontarf, Sigurd may have intended to make wide conquests on the island. Indeed, according to one twentieth-century authority on the battle, his hosting in 1014 'was an organised attempt at conquest, comparable to the attacks upon England, which in 1013 resulted in the occupation of that country'.[78]

77 *ASC*, 1013, 1014, 1015, 1016, 1017; *Brut Y Tywysogyon*, 1012–13, p. 11.   78 Goedheer, *Irish and Norse traditions about the Battle of Clontarf*, p. 105.

4 The Battle of Clontarf (Good Friday, 23 April 1014)

THE REVOLT OF KING BRIAN'S VASSALS

Despite the success of his campaigns, Brian's hold on the island was shaky in parts, especially in the north among the Cenél nEógain. He did have an acknowledged overlordship of the entire island, which was an astounding achievement for any medieval Irish king. Unsurprisingly, the first revolt against Brian's rule of Ireland came from the Cenél nEógain, led by Flaithbertach Ua Néill. In 1012, Flaithbertach began to attack his neighbours, the kings of Cenél Conaill and the Ulaid, having accepted Brian's overlordship for only two years.[1] Flaithbertach had been difficult enough to conquer in the first place, his having opposed Brian's attempts to impose overlordship on his kingdom from 1004 to 1010.[2] The kings whom Ua Néill attacked were also the high-king's vassals and they expected him to protect them from the depredations of the Cenél nEógain. Nevertheless, they seem to have remained loyal to Brian and did not join the rebellion. Brian sent his most powerful vassal, Máelsechnaill II, the king of Meath, to bring the northern king to heel. Although Máelsechnaill plundered the lands of the Cenel nEógain in 1012, even destroying the palace of the Ua Néill king at Tullaghoge, he was defeated and humiliated in 1013 when Flaithbertach raided deep into Meath.[3] The king of Cenél nEógain may also have orchestrated an attack on the high-king's major ally in the north of Ireland, Máel Muire the coarb of Patrick, by ordering the Conalli Muirtheimne dynasty of north Louth to defy the authority of the great monastery at Armagh by 'breaking' the relic, St Patrick's crozier or staff.[4]

In itself, the outbreak of Ua Néill's revolt in 1012 was not very serious. Indeed, Brian, being a thoughtful king, must have half expected such a

1 *AU*, 1012, 1013. 2 *AI*, 1005, 1006, 1007, 1010; *AU*, 1004, 1005, 1006, 1007, 1009, 1010.
3 *AU*, 1012, 1013. 4 *AFM*, 1012 [*recte* 1013]; *AU*, 1013.

reaction from that quarter. The northern revolt did become serious in 1013 when it continued into another year and the high-king's most important vassal, the king of Meath, was defeated. AU record that the king of Dublin, Sitric Silkenbeard, and Máelmórda, king of Leinster, took Máelsechnaill II's humiliation as the opportunity to launch their own challenge to Brian's overlordship. They did this by also attacking the kingdom of Meath. Sitric of Dublin must have been influenced by the success of the Viking invasions of the neighbouring kingdom of England. Perhaps he had had enough of Brian's overlordship and decided that he preferred to be under the patronage of a great Viking leader in England such as Svein Forkbeard, the king of Denmark.[5] Sitric's revolt was much more serious than that of Flaithbertach Ua Néill. The warriors of Dublin and Leinster defeated a raiding force from Máelsechnaill's army, killing 150 of the king of Meath's soldiers as well as his son Flann.[6] King Sitric also commanded 'a great fleet of the foreigners' led by his nephew Mathgamain (son of Dubgall, son of Amlaíb Cuarán, son of Sitric Cáech) to plunder the monastery and small Hiberno-Norse settlement at Cork. This Dublin raiding party was defeated in battle by a force led by the Uí Echach Muman dynasty. Sitric Silkenbeard's nephew and a number of other Scandinavian nobles were killed.[7] The tale recounted in *CGRG* of Gormlaith, Brian's queen, inciting her brother Máelmórda the king of Leinster to rebel – a tale embellished with gold-lined tunics, silver buttons and a fight over a board game like chess (*fidchell* or wood sense) – should be discounted for the fantasy that it is.[8] What is historical is the opportunity presented to the kings of Dublin and Leinster by the rebellion in the north, which Brian appeared to be failing adequately to suppress.

Although Brian may have erred in not treating the revolt of Flaithbertach Ua Néill with the respect and attention it deserved, in typical fashion he recovered from his initial mistake and decided to meet the rebellion of

5 *ASC*, 1013.   **6** *AU*, 1013.   **7** *AI*, 1013. The Annals of Inisfallen correctly identify the leader of this raid (see the Irish text on page 182). The editor and the other Irish annals, however, appear to have confused the original record by splitting Mathgamain's genealogy in half, making two Viking commanders out of the one originally intended. **8** *CGRG*, pp 142–7; Angela Gleason, 'Games' in Duffy (ed.), *Medieval Ireland*, p. 193.

Dublin and Leinster head on. Brian marched his army deep into Leinster in the autumn of 1013, where he remained close to Dublin from early September until Christmas.[9] His son Murchad was despatched on a dangerous mission to plunder in the Wicklow Mountains as far as Glendalough, and from there back to Kilmainham near Dublin.[10] Despite these efforts, the high-king's campaign 'did not bring about a peace' and he retired to Munster.[11]

Sitric knew that Brian would return more determined than ever at the start of 1014. As a result, he sailed for the main recruiting grounds for Viking warriors in the Irish Sea and the north of Britain, the Isle of Man and the jarldom of Orkney. It is quite possible that, as Njal's Saga recounts, Sitric Silkenbeard promised the kingdom of Ireland to both Sigurd Hlodvisson the jarl of Orkney and Brodir of Man, but it is impossible to be certain.[12] Sigurd raised a large force of warriors to accompany him to Dublin, probably many hundreds of heavily armed men. Brodir's force from the Isle of Man was probably smaller. No doubt he was still able to raise a substantial number of warriors. The Chronicle of the Princes records that 'Sitric, king of Dublin … hired longships and pirate ships full of armed men to assist him; and the leader of those was called Brodir'.[13] The Scandinavians probably agreed to be in Dublin by Palm Sunday 1014. Some historians state that Good Friday 1014 may not have been the exact date of the battle.[14] I can see no reason to doubt it. Such a date is easily remembered and would also have given the Munster army a possible edge in morale, the day being so important in the Christian calendar. By the week of Good Friday, the fleets from Orkney and Man had reached Dublin where the Scandinavian warriors were joined by the army of the king of Leinster. Dublin must have been full of hundreds of heavily armed warriors at this time. The Leinstermen most likely camped outside the town defences. For whatever reason, only the forces from the dynasties in the hinterland of Dublin (the Wicklow Mountains and the north-eastern plains of Kildare) joined the Leinster army. The Vikings gathered in Dublin

9 *AI*, 1013.   **10** *AU*, 1013.   **11** *AI*, 1013.   **12** *Njal's Saga*, pp 298–9.   **13** *Brut Y Tywysogyon*, 1014, p. 11.   **14** Ní Mhaonaigh, *Brian Boru*, p. 99.

21 Some Viking warrior pieces from the later twelfth-century Lewis chessmen. Jarl Sigurd and his men probably had round shields (© The Trustees of the British Museum).

formed a formidable army by any medieval standards, well armed in the Scandinavian manner.

Brian must have had intelligence of Sitric Silkenbeard's embassy to Orkney and Man and of the appointed time for the arrival of the Viking fleets at Dublin. As a result, he knew that he faced a very severe challenge. Evidence of this can be seen in the fact that the high-king fortified a number of strategic sites along the Shannon Estuary at Kincora, Inis Gaill Duib and Inis Locha Sainglenn, to guard the approaches to the Hiberno-Norse town of Limerick and his palace at Kincora. These fortifications have been identified as *Cathair Cinn Coradh*, 'the stone fort of Kincora at Killaloe', and 'the Island of the Black Foreigner', which may be an old name for King's Island at Limerick. The third site may refer to the environs of Singland Hill, which was just south of that town.[15] When the 1014

15 *AU*, 1013; *AI*, 1012; *AFM*, 1012 [*recte* 1013] (notes t, u, w).

campaigning season began, Brian mustered the forces still loyal to him on the island of Ireland and marched on Dublin. This comprised only the Munster army and a contingent from south Connacht. The south Connachtmen most likely joined Brian's army owing to the fact that his first wife Mór had been a daughter of Eiden son of Cléirech king of Uí Fhiachrach Aidne, and the mother of the high-king's most able son Murchad, who was to command the Munster army on the battlefield at Clontarf.[16] One of the kings from south Connacht was Murchad's first cousin, Máelruanaidh Ua hEidhin of Uí Fiachrach Aidne.[17] A second was Tadhg Ua Ceallaigh, the king of Uí Máine. Brian's army was still very large by medieval Irish standards, containing his own household troops, a large force of mercenaries, additional contributions from the Hiberno-Norse towns of Munster and the contingents of the Munster and south Connacht sub-kings. Brian's nobles and household troops, his mercenaries and his sub-kings and their followers would have been well armed in the Irish fashion and formed a large portion of the army. The contingents from the towns were also well armed, but in the Norse manner. The majority of Brian's Irish warriors were probably better equipped, trained and experienced than their equivalents in the armies of most other Irish kings.

The night of Holy Thursday, the high-king's army encamped at Clontarf after first having plundered and burned the Hiberno-Norse settlements in the vicinity of Dublin north of the Liffey. *CGRG* recounts a number of plausible events that may have taken place that night in King Brian's camp. It states that while in camp, Brian sent his son Donnchadh with a detachment of the Munster army to plunder Leinster 'in the absence of its people'.[18] This may have been done to unsettle the Leinster contingent of the opposing army and also to dissuade the dynasties in the south of the province from sending any reinforcements to Dublin. In addition, Donnchadh was half-brother to the king of Dublin and was also a nephew of the king of Leinster. The high-king and his favoured son Murchad may have felt that it was wise

---

16 O'Brien (ed.), *Corpus Genealogiarum Hiberniae*, 1, p. 238; Máire Ní Mhaonaigh, 'Brian Bóruma', *DIB*, 1, pp 829–32. **17** John O'Donovan (ed.), *The genealogies, tribes and customs of Hy-Fiachrach* (Dublin, 1844), p. 398. **18** *CGRG*, pp 154–5.

22 (*opposite*) Dál Cais warrior with crested helmet, spear and shield: a figure from the eleventh-century shrine of St Maelruain's Missal (courtesy of the National Museum of Ireland).

not to have Donnchadh in the battle line at Clontarf. If so, like many of Brian's actions, it was a shrewd move. The king of Meath, Máelsechnaill II, may also have been present in the camp the night before the battle. Again, according to *CGRG*, Máelsechnaill withdrew his force from the Munster army owing to treacherous communication with the rebels and a desire to gain strategic advantage over Brian.[19] Whatever occurred that night, Máelsechnaill and his soldiers did not take any part in the battle the next day. No casualties from Meath are recorded in any of the Irish annals. This would not have been the case had Máelsechnaill's army even participated in the pursuit of the remnants of the Viking–Leinster force from the River Tolka to the gates of Dublin, as recounted in AFM, which inserts the fable owing to its being a pro-Uí Néill source.[20]

There is no dispute as to where the Battle of Clontarf was fought.[21] Modern historians have placed it 'east of the Tolka' and south of Howth, on the small plain the medieval Irish called Mag n-Ealta.[22] This locates the battlefield in the present suburb of Dublin called Clontarf, which has held its name continuously since the era of the battle. As late as the 1830s, Clontarf was still 'a very richly wooded and finely cultivated country'.[23] At this time, 'the number of human bones discovered in excavating the ground for streets on the north side of Dublin' was so noteworthy as to be associated, rightly or wrongly, with the aftermath of the battle, and in Clontarf itself in the grounds of Danesfield House, 'a Danish sword was dug up in the garden in 1830'.[24] On an early nineteenth-century map, Danesfield House appears in the eastern part of Clontarf.[25] It is unclear, however, if

19 Ibid., pp 154–5, 168–9.   **20** *AFM*, 1013 [*recte* 1014].   **21** Ibid., note e; Ó hÓgáin, *Myth, legend and romance*, pp 55–7.   **22** John Ryan, 'The Battle of Clontarf', *JRSAI*, 68:1 (1938), 1–50; G.A. Hayes-McCoy, *Irish battles* (Belfast, 1969), pp 12–21.   **23** Samuel Lewis, *A topographical dictionary of Ireland*, 1 (1837), pp 376–7.   **24** Ibid.   **25** *Map of Clontarf, surveyed 1837*, OSI authorized internet map; see also *The Longfield Map Collection*, NLI MS 21F51, maps 081 (1792), 101 (1804), 115 (1812) and 141 (1816) – all of small parts of Clontarf.

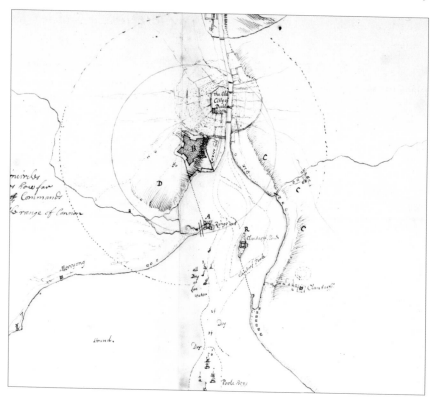

23 A section of one of the earliest surviving maps (1673) of Dublin Bay that illustrates the entire sweep of the Clontarf battlefield, stretching from Clontarf itself to the deep water at the Clontarf Pool and over the Tolka to Dubgall's Bridge. NMM MS 16P/49(10) (courtesy of the National Maritime Museum, UK).

Danesfield is an ancient place-name surviving from the time of the battle or a more recent one, given to the house that was prominent in the locality. The fact that a Viking sword may have been found there suggests that the area has some association with the battle.

The high-king and his army probably chose to encamp at Clontarf in 1014 because of the large Scandinavian forces assembled by Sitric Silkenbeard that made it too dangerous to locate any closer to Dublin. Brian may have been inspired to fight the next day, Good Friday, by the example of the famous German victory of Lechfeld, won in the year 955 by the Emperor Otto I (the Great) over an invading army of Magyar (Hungarian) horsemen. This battle began on 10 August, the feastday of St

Lawrence.[26] Like the German Emperor, Brian may have 'ordered his soldiers to perform vigils in memory of the saint [in 1014 Jesus himself] on the eve of the encounter'.[27] Lechfeld was the greatest battle that had taken place in Western or Central Europe during Brian's lifetime and it is possible that he was an admirer of the German emperors.

THE DAY OF BATTLE

Dolluid in beist, bág datha,
cucu trésin sál sithi;
Rind Chind Aíse, cia 'tchethe,
Aú Betha for Lind Liphi.

There came the beast, a pleasing combat,
toward them through the level sea:
the Point of Aes' Head, how should ye see it?
Bethe's Ear is over the Liffey-Pool.[28]

There seems no reason to doubt that on the morning of the battle the high-king delegated command of his army to his able son Murchad and retired behind the Munster battle line to pray. According to AU, Brian was born in 941, and, at the time of the battle, was 73 years of age, or very close to it. As such, he was too old to take an active part in the fighting.[29] Murchad was an accomplished warrior, having already led his father's army on campaign in the north of Ireland in 1011 and in Leinster in 1013.[30] He was also very loyal to his father, for many other Irish dynasts would have long deposed such an elderly king.[31] This fact is another testament to Brian's

---

26 Charles R. Bowlus, *The Battle of Lechfeld and its aftermath, August 955* (Aldershot, 2006), pp 1–7.   **27** Ibid., p. 2; Warner (ed. and trans.), *The Chronicon of Thietmar of Merseburg*, 955, pp 96–9.   **28** Edward Gwynn (ed.), *The Metrical Dindsenchas*, 3 (Dublin, 1913), pp 106–7, notes p. 495. A verse of a poem about Howth by the poet Cináed Ua hArtacáin (d. 975), recording the destruction wrought by a terrible sea monster in Dublin Bay.   **29** *AU*, 941.   **30** *AI*, 1011; *AU*, 1011, 1013; *Chronicle of the Princes* notes the prominent part played by Murchad in the 1014 campaign: *Brut Y Tywysogyon*, 1014, p. 11.   **31** In the year 1007, Murchad appears to have killed a trouble-

24 Crucifixion scene from the Sacramentary of the German Emperor Henry II, painted in Regensburg around the year 1012. Brian Boru, as 'Emperor of the Irish', may have been an admirer of the Ottonian emperors of Germany, and there appears to have been a definite imperial German influence on his high-kingship (Bayerische Staatsbibliothek München, Clm 4456, fo. 15r).

abilities and his success in managing his sons and wider family that greatly ensured the stability of his reign. Around sunrise on the morning of Good Friday 1014, the Munster army formed up facing towards Dublin. Murchad commanded the main portion of the royal army. The army most likely formed a large shield wall such as the Anglo-Saxons did at Hastings in 1066 against the Norman invaders of England. The well-equipped nobles and mercenaries would have been to the fore. *CGRG* and the Icelandic sagas tell of a Munster army composed of a central force and right and left wings commanded by various figures, some unidentifiable.[32] The high-king's army probably comprised one large body, commanded by Murchad, with his standards in the centre, surrounded by his household troops and nobles. Other than this armed mass having a left and right side including many more notable figures, everything else is speculation. A substantial force of well-armed men may also have been left behind to guard Brian, which formed itself into a second smaller shield wall or shieldburg as it is called in the Icelandic sagas.[33] Perhaps on the morning of the battle, as the high-king or Murchad (probably both) addressed their troops, the desertion of the Meathmen, if it had occurred, may have been used to further rouse and inspire the soldiers to fight long and hard for their king.

The alliance that sailed out of Dublin to face King Brian very early that morning was probably decidedly smaller than the Munster army. Nevertheless, the large battalion of heavily armed Vikings under the command of Sigurd the jarl of Orkney must have been very intimidating and a cause of grave concern to the leaders of the high-king's army. The majority of the Vikings were from the realm of Orkney, but there was also a substantial hosting from the Isle of Man, together with whatever well-armed troops were contributed to the forthcoming battle by Sitric Silkenbeard of Dublin. Apparently, Sitric did not join his army for the battle against Brian; according to *CGRG*, the king of Dublin watched the ensuing conflict from 'the battlements of his watch tower', a piece from this saga that may be factual.[34] The Irish force in the rebel army was that of

some south Connacht noble at the behest of his father: *AU*, 1007. **32** *CGRG*, pp 166–9; *Njal's Saga*, p. 301. **33** *Njal's Saga*, pp 301, 303; George Webbe Dasent (ed.), *The story of burnt Njal* (Edinburgh, 1861), ii, pp 334, 337. **34** *CGRG*, pp 190–1.

Máelmórda, king of Leinster. This contingent may have been fairly small and was led by Máelmórda and his north Leinster sub-king, Domnall of Fortuatha Laigen. While some of the leading nobles of the Leinster force would have been as well armed and equipped as Brian's best troops, they may have been few and the majority of the Leinstermen were probably not the equal of the Munster soldiery. This leads to the conclusion that Brian's army was larger and more evenly equipped to a high standard, while the Orkney element of the Viking–Leinster force was very well equipped and highly dangerous, but the other contingents possibly less so. When the rebel army landed from their ships on the beach at Clontarf, they formed up to face the high-king's warriors. Again, it probably comprised one large mass fronted by a shield wall to oppose the Munstermen. As was the case with Brian's army, many of the commanders of the Viking–Leinster force listed in the sagas are unidentifiable. The Icelandic sagas also recount that the Viking–Leinster army fought under the banner of Jarl Sigurd of Orkney that Orkneyinga Saga calls 'the raven banner'.[35] This is another saga tradition about the Battle of Clontarf that may actually be true. Raven banners are recorded elsewhere as being captured from Viking armies in England. Cnut of Denmark in 1016 was reputed to have had a raven banner at the Battle of Ashingdon.[36] This type of standard was inspired by Norse mythology, the raven being a bird closely associated with Odin, the Scandinavian god of war.[37]

The historian G.A. Hayes-McCoy in the mid-twentieth century researched the Battle of Clontarf and came to the conclusion that 'the total strength of both sides added together did not exceed 5,000 men',[38] a figure that I believe to be a very good estimate. Saga accounts of the battle state that it began at sunrise and continued into the evening, 'the same length of time as that which the tide takes to go, and to flood, and to fill'.[39] (In 1861, Dr Samuel Haughton, professor of Geology at TCD, calculated for James Henthorn Todd, the editor and translator of *CGRG*, that 'the tide along the

35 *Njal's Saga*, p. 302; *Orkneyinga Saga*, p. 38. 36 Alistair Campbell (ed.), *Encomium Emmae Reginae* (Cambridge, 1998), pp 24–5. 37 Roesdahl, *The Vikings*, pp 144–5, 149–50. 38 Hayes–McCoy, *Irish battles*, p. 16. 39 *CGRG*, pp 190–1.

25 'Battle of Clontarf' by the Irish landscape artist Hugh Frazer (1826). This painting shows a familiarity with elements of both *Cogadh Gaedhel re Gallaibh* and Njal's Saga (courtesy of the Isaacs Art Center, Hawaii).

Clontarf shore' was full at 5.30am on Good Friday morning in 1014 and was full again in the evening at 5.55pm).[40] While it is unknown if this given length of the battle is correct, in the eleventh century when two elite forces used to success in battle, such as King Brian's Munster and south Connacht army and Sigurd's men from Orkney, encountered each other on the battlefield, fighting could indeed last for many hours. The Battle of Hastings, fought on Saturday 14 October 1066 between another two such forces, the recently victorious Anglo-Saxon army of King Harold Godwinson and the ducal forces of William the 'Bastard' of Normandy, is also said to have continued for most of the day, from 9am 'until twilight'.[41]

40 Ibid., pp xxvi–xxvii; Samuel Haughton and James Henthorn Todd, *The tides of Dublin Bay and the Battle of Clontarf, 23rd April 1014* (Dublin, 1861), pp 1–3. **41** M.K.

Medieval battles commenced with combats between accomplished warriors from both sides and no doubt the conflict at Clontarf was little different. According to *CGRG*, the first champion to step forward for Brian's army was Domnall son of Eimen *mormaer* of Mar and that his opponent from the Viking–Leinster army was a Scandinavian or Orcadian warrior called Plait.[42] The words said to have been exchanged between the two champions are recorded in *CGRG*. The night before the battle, Plait is reputed to have boasted 'that there was not a man in Erin who was able to fight him', hence the selection of the Scottish Gael Domnall to oppose him.[43] As the shield walls faced each other that morning on the Clontarf battlefield, Plait is said to have emerged from his lines and shouted three times '*Far as Domhnall?*', 'Where is Domnall?', three words that are a good attempt by the author of *CGRG* to record the Old Norse phrase '*hvar es Dufnal?*'.[44] *CGRG* states that *Mormaer* Domnall replied '*Sund, a sniding*' (Old Norse *niðingr*), 'Here, thou knave', and also records that the warriors ended up killing each other, an outcome that was probably a common result of these combats.[45] Although this is a good story and the *Mormaer* Domnall would have been an excellent choice to commence the fighting for Brian's army, we may never know if this passage from *CGRG* about the start of the battle is true. The fact that *CGRG* refers to Domnall's opponent Plait as 'son of the king of Lochlainn' suggests that this man's origins, even if the name is possibly correct, were either unknown to the Irish or had been forgotten.[46] As I will demonstrate, some of the information about the end of the battle in the Irish and Icelandic sagas may be accurate.

At some stage, the shield walls advanced and the battle became a general mêlée. This phase of the battle may have been prolonged, as relatives, friends and adherents placed themselves between their leaders and the advancing opponents before being cut down and replaced by more members of the army. There is no reason to doubt the accounts of the

Lawson, *The Battle of Hastings, 1066* (Stroud, 2007), pp 15, 62, 113–14, 120, 125–97. **42** *CGRG*, pp 174–7. **43** Ibid., pp 174–5. **44** Ibid., n. 16. **45** Ibid., pp 176–7; Donnchadh Ó Corráin, 'Old Norse and medieval Irish: bilingualism in Viking-Age Dublin' in Bradley, Fletcher and Simms (eds), *Dublin in the medieval world*, p. 67. **46** *CGRG*, pp 174–7.

26 Book of Kells: Irish warrior with shield throwing a spear. Note the warrior's unusual throwing style (detail from fo. 99v, courtesy of the Board of Trinity College Dublin).

actual fighting recounted in *CGRG*, Njal's Saga and Orkneyinga Saga, with warriors' hair and body parts being cut off, and many men surrounding the main commanders being killed. Both Njal's Saga and Orkneyinga Saga describe men being killed surrounding the jarl of Orkney's banner, which is believable, even if the legends recounted are apocryphal.[47] Similarly, the scene of Brian asking his servant to follow the progress of Murchad's standard throughout the battle could very easily have happened.[48] What is not clear is how the Munster army gained the upper hand, which evidently it did as the battle progressed. As we have seen, Irish warriors in medieval times were said to fight in battle without wearing any metal armour. This raises the important question as to how the Munster soldiers overcame the heavily armed and armoured Vikings from Orkney, Man and Dublin on the Clontarf battlefield. Large volleys of spears thrown by the Munster warriors must have been very effective against the massed ranks of the Viking shield wall. Njal's Saga recounts how the jarl of Orkney was killed by an Irish spear.[49] I suspect that the Scandinavians who fought in the

47 *Njal's Saga*, p. 302; *Orkneyinga Saga*, p. 38.   48 *CGRG*, pp 196–201.   49 *Njal's Saga*, p. 302.

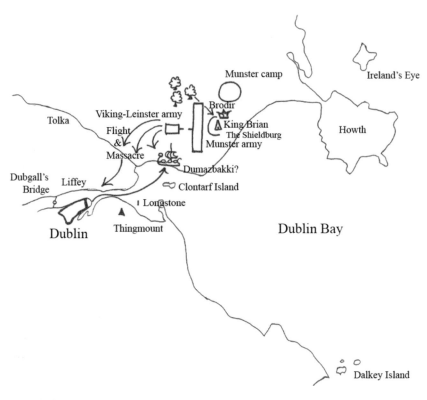

27 Map of the Clontarf battlefield (not to scale; based upon author's research).

Battle of Clontarf were heavily outnumbered by the high-king's soldiers, and individuals or small groups of Vikings may have become isolated on the battlefield, surrounded by Munster warriors and hacked to death through sheer force of numbers.

The jarl of Orkney was killed, which appears to have been a major event in the battle. A third Icelandic saga, Thorstein's Saga, which has a very short account of the Battle of Clontarf, records that, just before he was killed, Jarl Sigurd was advised to retreat to *Dumazbakki*, the sandbank or the sanddune.[50] This was possibly where the jarl and his army had left their ships. It is believed, however, that the incoming tide in Dublin Bay on the evening of the Battle of Clontarf was an unusually high neap tide, and that

---

50 Benjamin Hudson, 'Brjáns Saga' in *Irish Sea studies*, pp 151–2.

this caused the Viking longships (many of which were probably fairly small) to float off from where they had been beached.[51] This trapped the fleeing Viking warriors, who were either drowned as they attempted to swim to their ships or slaughtered on the beach by the Munster soldiers. An almost-contemporary record of this massacre on the beach was made by the Frankish chronicler Ademar of Chabannes, who wrote between the years 1015 and 1033.[52] The fighting at the end of the battle surrounding the commander of the Munster army, Murchad, the high-king's son, also appears to have been fierce. Murchad was mortally wounded. The many casualties among Brian's family and the Munster nobility and sub-kings suggest that they fell fighting around Murchad. Only the advance of the jarl of Orkney's force could have inflicted such carnage, and it may be that the elite section of Brian's army commanded by Murchad fought the Scandinavians under the jarl of Orkney. It is testament to the fighting qualities of the high-king's family and retainers that it appears that they eventually won through, although they suffered appalling casualties. Murchad appears to have died of his wounds the morning after the battle ended.[53]

CGRG and the Icelandic sagas cannot be relied upon for their accounts of the battle, but the passages that deal with the death of King Brian do have a sense of authenticity. A section of Njal's Saga indicates that the men of the shieldburg protecting Brian left to join the battle.[54] If this force was substantial and left suddenly in a group, they could have been the deciding factor that forced the survivors of the Viking–Leinster army to flee. All this, however, is speculation. Although one can never know, one can picture Brian following the battle and then letting loose his bodyguards at the decisive moment. If he did, it was to prove to be his undoing. As a result, the Scandinavian noble Brodir and possibly a few followers managed to gain access to the high-king's position. The two saga traditions differ

51 Haughton and Todd, *The tides of Dublin Bay and the Battle of Clontarf*, pp 2–3; *Orkneyinga Saga*, p. 65. **52** The record in Ademar's Chronicon is a little confused but essentially correct: Bourgain (ed.), 'Ademari Cabannensis Chronicon', 1014, p. 173 (notes p. 306). **53** *CGRG*, pp 196–7. **54** *Njal's Saga*, p. 303.

slightly in detail, but substantially agree as to how this occurred. According to Njal's Saga, Brodir was hiding in some trees having been bested during the fighting and he made a deliberate and determined attack on the high-king once he saw Brian's bodyguards move off.[55] CGRG recounts that Brodir and two of his men found Brian by accident while roaming behind where the Munster shield wall had been, after holding their ground and being left behind as the rest of the Viking–Leinster army broke and fled and were pursued by the high-king's warriors.[56] What is common to both tales is that Brodir got access to Brian across a by-then largely empty main battle-field that contained only the dead and wounded.[57] Whichever was the case, a determined assault on King Brian was made. The few retainers with the high-king were probably young servants and most were quickly killed. Brian may have defended himself with his sword and gravely injured Brodir, but he was struck in the head and killed.[58] If the account so far is accurate, there is no reason to doubt that some of Brian's servants escaped and ran to the nearest Munster troops to tell them that an attack was under way on their king. When they arrived back, however, it was too late. It seems clear that Brodir was captured and executed, although it may not have been in the gory manner recorded in the sagas.[59] There is nothing in the saga accounts of the death of the high-king that contradicts the chronicle entry written by the Irish monk Marianus Scottus, probably before the year 1072, that states that 'Brian, king of Ireland' was killed in 1014 while preparing for Easter 'with his hands and mind directed towards God'.[60] 'Brian's sword' later ended up in the possession of the king of Leinster, Diarmait mac Máel na mBó, who possibly took it from the Dubliners some time after he seized control of their town in 1052.[61]

CGRG states that Brian's grandson Turlough was killed during the pursuit of the fleeing remnants of the Viking–Leinster army, drowned as he fought hand-to-hand with some Vikings at the weir of Clontarf.[62] It is a

55 Ibid. **56** *CGRG*, pp 202–3. **57** Ibid.; *Njal's Saga*, p. 303. **58** *CGRG*, pp 202–3. **59** *Njal's Saga*, p. 303. **60** G. Waitz (ed.), 'Mariani Scotti Chronicon', *Monumenta Germaniae Historica*, 5 (Hanover, 1844), 1014, p. 555 (www.mgh.de). **61** *AI*, 1068; *AU*, 1052; Diarmait mac Máel na mBó may have been something of a collector of famous swords. **62** *CGRG*, pp 192–3.

28 Dál Cais warrior with sword, sitting on a wolf-dog throne, a figure from the eleventh-century shrine of St Maelruain's Missal. Could this figure be a depiction of King Brian drawing his sword at Clontarf to defend himself against Brodir? (courtesy of the National Museum of Ireland).

plausible story, although we can never know if it is accurate. There may also be some truth to another passage at the end of *CGRG* that states that it was the 'household troops of Tadhg Ua Ceallaigh (*lucht tighe Taidg Ui Cellaig*)' who gave chase to the fugitives from the Viking–Leinster army that attempted to escape to the safety of Dublin by fording the Tolka and then crossing Dubgall's Bridge over the Liffey.[63] An ancient if garbled tradition from Kilmainham suggests that some of the casualties from the battle were buried at the church of St Maignenn, but among them was believed to be Tadhg Ua Ceallaigh.[64] This seems possible, if he was killed near Dubgall's Bridge. King Sitric's nephew, Gilla Ciaráin, may also have been interred here.[65] This passage from *CGRG* also contains an intriguing statement that the last Viking killed was called Arnaill Scot, who, as the nineteenth-

63 Ibid., pp 184–5.   64 *The antiquities and history of Ireland by the Right Honourable Sir James Ware, knt.* (London, 1705), p. 64.   65 Ibid.

29 Nineteenth-century print entitled 'After the Battle of Clontarf Brian Boru is killed by Brodir, a Dane'. It is based on the account of the death of King Brian in Njal's Saga (courtesy of the National Library of Ireland).

century editor of *CGRG* correctly suggested, could be the 'Arnljot' referred to in Njal's Saga as Jarl Sigurd's 'man in charge' of the island of Stroma, the final Orkney island in the Pentland Firth before the Scottish mainland.[66]

Any figures given for the casualties inflicted on the two armies in the Battle of Clontarf are estimates. The attrition rate of leaders on both sides was heavy. The pursuit of the fleeing remnants of an army in medieval times could degenerate into a massacre, especially if an unexpected natural phenomenon occurred at the same time, such as the unusually high neap tide at Clontarf in 1014, or thunderstorms and flash-flooding as at Lechfeld in 955.[67] This suggests that the Viking–Leinster army suffered severe casualties at Clontarf, especially if part of the army had been trapped along the seashore or along the banks of the Tolka or the Liffey. The Munster army also suffered large casualties, which led AU to describe the battle as 'a valiant battle … the like of which was never encountered'.[68] In fact, the losses were so severe as to make Clontarf a pyrrhic victory for the Munstermen.

There are extensive lists of those killed in the Battle of Clontarf in the Irish annals. The names given are readily identifiable and quite accurate. Those killed from the Munster army are headed by King Brian, his son Murchad and Murchad's son Turlough. The reference to the death of the high-king in AU, where he is called 'the Augustus of the whole of north-west Europe – *August iartair tuaiscirt Eorpa uile*', is probably due to Brian's use of the title 'Emperor of the Irish' and German Ottonian influences on his high-kingship.[69] Also killed were Conaing, Brian's nephew, and Eochu, Niall and Cúduiligh (one of Brian's grandnephews – the son of Cennétig son of Donncuan, d. 948, son of Cennétig, d. 951), who were known as 'Brian's three guards' or 'the three rear-guards of Brian'.[70] (These three were possibly the high-king's personal bodyguards.) Five Munster sub-kings – Mothla, king of

66 *CGRG*, pp clxxxi, 184–7; *Njal's Saga*, p. 139; *Orkneyinga Saga*, map of Orkney and Caithness. 67 Bowlus, *The Battle of Lechfeld and its aftermath*, pp 97–154. 68 *AU*, 1014. 69 Ibid. 70 Ibid.; *AFM*, 1013 [*recte* 1014] (notes k, 1), 948; *CGRG*, pp 166–7, 208–9; Ryan, 'The Battle of Clontarf', p. 42; O'Brien (ed.), *Corpus Genealogiarum Hiberniae*, i, pp 237–8; *AI*, 951.

Déisi Muman, Mac Beatha, king of Ciarraige Luachra, Scannlan, king of Eóganacht Locha Léin, Geibheannach, king of Fernmag (Fermoy), and Domnall, king of Corco Baiscind – were also slain along with two sub-kings from south Connacht, Tadhg Ua Ceallaigh, king of Uí Máine and Máelruanaidh Ua hEidhin, king of Uí Fiachrach Aidne, another of Brian's nephews.[71] The Scottish Gaelic nobleman Domnall son of Eimen son of Cainnech *mormaer* of Mar was also killed fighting for Brian.[72] Almost the entire leadership of the Viking–Leinster army was killed. Their casualty list is headed by Sigurd Hlodvisson the Stout jarl of Orkney, Brodir of Man, Amlaíb, son of Lagmann, who was probably a Hebridean chieftain, Óttarr the Black (possibly another Scandinavian noble from the Isle of Man), King Sitric's brother, Dubgall, and his nephew, Gilla Ciaráin, Donnchadh Ua Eruilb, a member of a wealthy Dublin family, King Máelmórda of Leinster and Domnall, king of Fortuatha Laigen.[73] AI recount the slaughter of the 'foreigners of the western world' in its description of the battle.[74]

It is striking that no kings from the Munster dynasties who had opposed the rise of Brian and the Dál Cais, such as the Uí Echach Muman branch of the Eóganacht, are recorded in the Irish annals as having been killed on the battlefield at Clontarf.[75] Perhaps Brian's son Donnchadh took them with him on his diversionary raid into Leinster, evidence of yet another probable shrewd decision by the high-king and Murchad. AFM also have confused references to two additional Leinster casualties in their account of the battle that are unreliable. One of those mentioned, Tuathal, son of Augaire of the south Kildare Uí Muiredaig dynasty, was actually a king of Leinster who died over fifty years before the Battle of Clontarf in 958.[76] Even if Tuathal's son, Dúnlaing, was the intended figure, this is also an error. Although *CGRG* states that Dúnlaing was beheaded during the fighting at Clontarf, in reality

---

71 *AU*, 1014; *AI*, 1014; *AFM*, 1013 [*recte* 1014].   **72** *AU*, 1014.   **73** Ibid., 1014; Clarke, 'Sitriuc Silkbeard', *DIB*, 8, p. 976; Downham, *Viking kings of Britain and Ireland*, pp 251–2; David E. Thornton, 'Clann Eruilb: Irish or Scandinavian', *IHS*, 30:118 (1996), 161–6. A powerful family of Manx jarls was using the personal name Ótarr in the eleventh century: George Broderick (ed.), Chronica regum manniae et insularum: *Chronicles of the kings of Man and the Isles* (Douglas, 2004), fo. 34r.   **74** *AI*, 1014.   **75** Ibid., 1014, 1015; *AU*, 1014, 1015; *AFM*, 1013 [*recte* 1014].   **76** *AFM*, 1013 [*recte* 1014] (note y); *AU*, 958.

he died of old age at Glendalough in the immediate aftermath of the battle, having briefly succeeded Máelmórda as king of Leinster.[77] The other reference in AFM is to the death of Brogarbhan, son of Conchobar, king of Uí Failge, during the battle and this record is probably also incorrect.[78] It is unlikely that there were many warriors from Uí Muiredaig or Uí Failge in the Leinster contingent at Clontarf. The south Leinster Uí Cheinnselaig dynasty was almost certainly not represented at the battle, although *CGRG* lists them as part of the force of Leinstermen at Clontarf.[79] *CGRG* also includes the complete fantasy that a king of Bréifne called Fergal Ua Ruairc turned up to join Brian's army at Clontarf, leading the men of Bréifne and Conmaicne under a 'gold-spangled banner', 'that had gained victory in every battle and every conflict, and in every combat'.[80] Although Fergal Ua Ruairc is a historical figure, he died in 966.[81] It is fitting that, in the account of the Battle of Clontarf given in *CGRG*, his fictional battalion is said to have fought the warriors from Uí Muiredaig and Uí Cheinnselaig, who were probably not present on the battlefield either.[82]

THE AFTERMATH

AU record that the royal dead of the Munster army were taken to the monastery of Swords, just north of Clontarf. There Máel Muire, the coarb of Armagh, a supporter of Brian and the head of the church that the high-king had done so much to promote as the ecclesiastical capital of Ireland, took the king's body and also the body of his son Murchad, the head of his nephew Conaing and that of Mothla, the king of the Déisi, to Armagh for burial 'in a new tomb'. A ceremonial wake was held at Armagh 'for twelve

77 *CGRG*, pp 176–7; *AU*, 1014.   **78** *AFM*, 1013 [*recte* 1014] (note x); see n. 2 on p. 11 of *ALC*, 1014, for a possible reason for the confusion of the writers of the Annals of the Four Masters with this name. *AFM* is a later compilation by a generation and used *ALC* as one of its sources. The Four Masters appear to have suspected that there was something wrong with their references to the deaths of these two figures and hence the confusion in their account.   **79** *CGRG*, pp 164–5, 176–7.   **80** Ibid., pp 156–7, 176–7.   **81** *AU*, 966.   **82** *CGRG*, pp 176–7; Byrne, *Irish kings and high-kings*, p. 299.

30 The early medieval cross-shaft in the graveyard of St Maignenn's Church in Kilmainham, Dublin (courtesy of the OPW; photograph by Frank McGettigan).

nights ... in honour of the dead king'.[83] Tadhg Ua Ceallaigh, the king of Uí Máine, may have been buried 'near the old stone cross', at the church of St Maignenn in Kilmainham.[84] *CGRG* indicates that Brian's other son, Donnchadh, arrived back in camp on Easter Sunday to lead the battered remnants of the Munster army, including the many wounded, back to the southern kingdom.[85] If the passages from *CGRG* and Njal's Saga are accurate (which I think they substantially are), then Brian died well. He also died as he lived, as high-king of Ireland. If Gerald of Wales, the historian of the twelfth-century Anglo-Norman invasion of Ireland, can be believed, the last true high-king, Rory Ua Conchobair, king of Connacht, was caught bathing in the Liffey at the siege of Dublin in 1171 and fled from the battlefield, leaving the high-kingship of Ireland behind him.[86]

83 *AU*, 1014.   **84** *The antiquities and history of Ireland*, p. 64; *AFM*, 1013 [*recte* 1014] (second note b); Gwynn and Hadcock, *Medieval religious houses Ireland*, p. 334.   **85** *CGRG*, pp 210–11; Waitz (ed.), 'Mariani Scotti Chronicon', 1014, p. 555.   **86** A.B. Scott and F.X. Martin (eds), *Expugnatio Hibernica: The conquest of Ireland by Giraldus*

The decline in the fortunes of the Dál Cais after the Battle of Clontarf was sudden and dramatic. Donnchadh, who appears to have been the preferred successor to King Brian, was immediately opposed and defeated in battle by his half-brother Tadhg.[87] In 1016, the Dál Cais suffered the indignity of watching an army from Connacht destroy Brian's palace at Kincora.[88] Although AI record that in 1016 Donnchadh became king of Munster when he 'took the hostages of Munster from Cnámhchaill westwards',[89] in 1019 Donnchadh was almost assassinated when Domnall son of Cathrannach, one of the Uí Chaisíne (a leading rival family of the Dál Cais excluded from the kingship by Brian's family), struck him on the head with the glancing blow of a sword that 'chanced on his right hand, straightaway cutting it off at the base of the thumb in that place'.[90] The assassin was executed 'immediately in that spot'.[91]

After the Battle of Clontarf, Máelsechnaill II of Meath retook the high-kingship of Ireland. He was supported in his resumed high-kingship by Flaithbertach Ua Néill, king of Cenél nEógain. In 1015, Flaithbertach 'went into Meath to assist Máelsechnaill', and together the two Uí Néill kings 'went on an expedition into Leinster, plundered it, and brought away a great tribute in cows and the pledges of the Leinstermen'.[92] In their entry for the next year, AU record that Brian's legacy continued into the reign of Máelsechnaill, with Ireland in 1016 largely 'at peace'.[93] Máelsechnaill II died on 2 September 1022, 'in the 43rd year of his reign and the 73rd of his age', 'dead from a drink of mead' (*marb di óul meda*).[94] Like Brian, Máelsechnaill II, upon his death, was apparently greatly mourned in Ireland. AFM record that 'sorrowful to the poor of the Lord was the death of Máelsechnaill', adding that 'most of the seniors [the most important clergy] of Ireland, were present [at his death]'.[95]

According to the ancient traditions of the high-kingship, Flaithbertach Ua Néill should have succeeded Máelsechnaill II as high-king. He does not

Cambrensis (Dublin, 1978), pp 78–85. **87** *AU*, 1014. **88** *AFM*, 1015 [*recte* 1016]. **89** *AI*, 1016. **90** Ibid., 1016; Ryan, 'The Dalcassians', 200. **91** *AI*, 1016. **92** *AU*, 1015. **93** Ibid., 1016. **94** Ibid., 1022; *AI*, 1022; Kevin Murray (ed.), *Baile in Scáil: 'The Phantom's Frenzy'* (Dublin, 2004), pp 47, 65. **95** *AFM*, 1022.

appear to have done so. When he died in 1036, 'of a tumour in a monastery' (*bebais éc atbai hi táilcentaig*), AU refer to him as 'high-king of Aileach', by which they mean he was king of Cenél nEógain only.[96] For the year 1018, AFM record 'a war between Máelsechnaill and the Uí Néill of the north'. The entry further states that the Cenél nEógain 'went northwards over Sliabh-Fuaid', a mountain in modern Co. Armagh. This record probably indicates that Flaithbertach Ua Néill fell out with Máelsechnaill II in that year and took his army home to Cenél nEógain.[97] Certainly, Ua Néill was active in the north the next year, 1019, when he plundered Tír Enda and Tír Lughdhach in Cenél Conaill.[98] Therefore, the cooperation between Máelsechnaill II and Flaithbertach Ua Néill after Clontarf may have lasted for only four years, which was a typical length of time at this period for cooperation between rival Irish kings to endure. In any event, the Clann Cholmáin and the rest of the Southern Uí Néill refused to support Flaithbertach Ua Néill in the bid he made to become high-king of Ireland after the death of Máelsechnaill II in 1022.

Ua Néill did make an attempt to become high-king. In 1025, he led his army into Brega and 'took the hostages of the Irish from the foreigners'.[99] When Flaithbertach returned to Meath early the next year, he 'took hostages' from the Southern Uí Néill and made good use of the very cold winter to cross 'thick ice' and capture Inis Mochta, an island in a small lake near Slane (now Inishmot, Co. Meath). The church on Inis Mochta had been seized and fortified as a base by a force of Vikings.[1] Once it became apparent that he would never become high-king, Ua Néill retired as king of Cenél nEógain, although he later resumed his kingship in 1034.[2] In 1030, Ua Néill left Ireland to go on pilgrimage to Rome.[3] Upon his return in 1031, he was known as Flaithbertach *an Trostáin* (of the pilgrim's staff), owing to his travels.[4] Despite never becoming high-king, Flaithbertach Ua Néill did have a successful reign as king of Cenél nEógain. AFM liken the reign of

96 Murray (ed.), *Baile in Scáil*, pp 47, 66; *AU*, 1036.   **97** *AFM*, 1017 [*recte* 1018]. **98** *AU*, 1019.   **99** Ibid., 1025.   **1** Ibid., 1026; *AFM*, 922 (note c), 1026.   **2** *AI*, 1034; see also Murray (ed.), *Baile in Scáil*, pp 4–7, 29–30.   **3** *AI*, 1029; *AU*, 1030.   **4** *AU*, 1031; Ailbhe MacShamhráin, 'Flaithbertach Ua Néill', *DIB*, 9, pp 598–9; *AFM*, 1036.

Ua Néill to that of Brian Boru, when times were good and a 'very great bargain used to be got at Armagh'. The Four Masters include the following poem to illustrate this:

> *Seisedhach do ghrán corca,*
> *No train dáirnibh dubh corcra,*
> *No do dercnaibh darach duinn,*
> *No do cnoibh falach fionncuill.*
> *Fogaibhthe gan tacha tinn,*
> *In Ard Macha ar aon pinginn.*

> A measure of oaten grain,
> Or a third of [a measure of] black-red sloes,
> Or of the acorns of the brown oak,
> Or of the nuts of the fair hazel-hedge,
> Was got without stiff bargaining,
> At Armagh, for one *pinginn* [a penny's worth of silver].[5]

The career of Brian's son Donnchadh improved somewhat after the death of Máelsechnaill II. His greatest rival, his half-brother, Tadhg, was removed from the scene when 'treacherously slain' in 1023.[6] In 1026, Donnchadh took the hostages of the Southern Uí Néill and the Leinstermen and 'he himself spent three days in Áth Cliath without opposition with his camp nearby the fort'.[7] An inscription on the *cumdach* or shrine of St Maelruain's Missal that was made between 1026 and 1033 and is associated with the Dál Cais, refers to Donnchadh at this time, with some exaggeration as 'king of Ireland'. The full inscription reads *Oroit do Dondchad Macc Briain do Rig Herend*, which translates as 'A prayer for Donnchadh son of Brian, king of Ireland'.[8] In 1040, he passed a remarkable law that seems to have been promulgated all over Ireland:

5 *AFM*, 1031. In medieval Ireland, a *pinginn* of silver was equal to 'the weight of seven grains of wheat': ibid., note n. **6** *AI*, 1023. **7** Ibid., 1026; *AU*, 1026. **8** Pádraig Ó Riain, 'The shrine of the Stowe Missal, redated', *PRIA*, 91C10 (1991), 285–7; O'Neill, *The Irish hand*, pp 6–7.

31 (*opposite*) The shrine of St Maelruain's Missal, a piece of eleventh-century metalwork associated with King Brian's son, Donnchadh. The silver cross encrusted with rock crystals is a later fourteenth-century addition. Much of the imagery on the shrine is associated with Good Friday and possibly the Battle of Clontarf. Note the crucifixion scene on the cover (courtesy of the National Museum of Ireland).

to the effect that none should dare steal, or do feats of arms on Sunday, or go out on Sunday carrying any load; and furthermore, that none should dare fetch cattle within doors.[9]

Donnchadh's last years as king of Munster were blighted by serious opposition from family rivals, led by Tadhg's son, Turlough, who had the support of the powerful king of Leinster, Diarmait mac Máel na mBó. Turlough launched his rebellion in 1053 and, along with Mac Máel na mBó, inflicted a severe defeat on Donnchadh at the Battle of Sliabh Crot, fought at the eastern entrance to the Glen of Aherlow in 1058.[10] The town of Limerick was set on fire during this campaign.[11] Donnchadh retained the title of king of Munster afterwards, but his power was broken. In 1063, 'Turlough Ua Briain took the kingship of Munster'.[12] Donnchadh abdicated and the next year 'went to Rome' on pilgrimage.[13] Donnchadh died in Rome in 1064, 'in the monastery of Stephen the martyr' (probably the modern San Lorenzo fuori le Mura, where St Stephen is reputed to be buried and which was an important destination for pilgrims visiting Rome in medieval times), according to AFM.[14]

Brian's queen Gormlaith died in the year 1030.[15] She possibly was 'a very beautiful woman' but may not have deserved her sinister reputation that is evident in the Irish and Icelandic sagas.[16] Evil or wronged women were stock characters of many medieval sagas and legends, from a wide variety of cultures. The characters served to allow medieval authors present the often complex reasons behind important events in a simple and concise manner that appealed to their audiences. It is unclear when Brian's daughter, Sláine,

9 *AI*, 1040. **10** *AU*, 1058; *AFM*, 1058 (note y). **11** *AI*, 1058. **12** Ibid., 1063. **13** Ibid., 1064; *AU*, 1064. **14** *AU*, 1064; *AFM*, 1064. **15** *AI*, 1030; *AFM*, 1030. **16** *Njal's Saga*, pp 296–7; *CGRG*, pp 142–3.

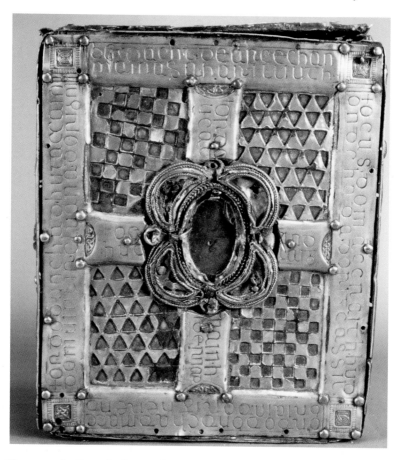

32 The prayer for Donnchadh son of Brian inscribed on the underside of the shrine of St Maelruain's Missal (courtesy of the National Museum of Ireland).

who was married to Sitric Silkenbeard, died. According to *CGRG*, Sitric 'became angered and gave her a blow', while they were watching the Battle of Clontarf from the battlements of his tower in Dublin. Sláine is said to have commented 'The foreigners are going into the sea, their natural inheritance'.[17] Brian's other married daughter, Bebhinn, died at an advanced age in 1073. AFM state that she 'died on her pilgrimage at Armagh', a record that suggests that Bebhinn continued to live among the Cenél nEógain in

17 *CGRG*, pp 192–3.

the north of Ireland long after the death of her husband, King Flaithbertach Ua Néill, in 1036.[18] She probably did so in an effort to support the careers of the children she had together with Ua Néill.

THE AFTERMATH IN THE SCANDINAVIAN WORLD

The carnage at Clontarf had a major impact in the Scandinavian world. Some historians argue that the jarldom of Orkney never fully recovered from the death of Jarl Sigurd the Stout at the battle in 1014. Sigurd's death is said to mark 'the end of an age', with great interference in the jarldom's affairs in the years after Clontarf by the kings of Norway.[19] The jarldom of Orkney was split for a long time after 1014 among Sigurd Hlodvisson's four sons. This led to rivalry, murder and even 'serious famine' in parts of Orkney.[20] When Sigurd the Stout's youngest son, Thorfinn, became sole jarl around the year 1030, the Orkney realm saw a further destructive war between Thorfinn and his nephew Rognvald Brusason, who had the backing of the king of Norway, Magnus the Good (king from 1035 to 1047).[21] Thorfinn Sigurdarson won out in around 1045 only when he managed to surprise Rognvald on the small island of Papa Stronsay in the Orkneys and have him killed.[22] Thorfinn then ruled Orkney alone, unchallenged until his death, probably around the year 1058.[23] The later years of his rule were a much greater success, with little further interference from Norway. Although the Icelandic sagas refer to Thorfinn as 'Thorfinn the Mighty', they are probably exaggerating when they say that he was more powerful than his father.[24] After Thorfinn's death, the power of the Orkney jarldom quickly crumbled and never recovered. Like many of his contemporaries among the Irish kings, Jarl Thorfinn is reputed to have made a

---

18 *AFM*, 1073; *AU*, 1073. **19** Forte, Oram and Pedersen (eds), *Viking empires*, pp 271–7. **20** *Orkneyinga Saga*, pp 38–56. **21** Ibid., pp 56–76. **22** Ibid., pp 70–1. **23** Woolf, *From Pictland to Alba*, p. 309. **24** *Orkneyinga Saga*, p. 224; Forte, Oram and Pedersen (eds), *Viking empires*, pp 271–3; Woolf, *From Pictland to Alba*, p. 244.

pilgrimage to Rome shortly after he finally won the war for control of Orkney.[25]

The wily Sitric Silkenbeard remained in power as king of Dublin for a further twenty-two years after the Battle of Clontarf. Sitric appears to have used the opportunity presented by the death of King Brian to recommence raiding for slaves in Dublin's hinterland.[26] After Clontarf, Sitric's relations with the Leinstermen deteriorated. He blinded the king of Leinster, Máelmórda's son, Bran (his own first cousin), in 1018, and was defeated at the Battle of Delgany by Augaire, king of Leinster, in 1021.[27] Nevertheless, it is probable that in these years Sitric secured the patronage of Cnut, the king of England, Denmark and Norway.[28] Cnut returned to invade England in 1015 with a fleet of 160 ships and by October 1016 ended most Anglo-Saxon resistance when he defeated the army of Æthelred's son, Edmund, at the Battle of Ashingdon in Essex.[29] Æthelred the *Unraed* died on 23 April 1016, two years to the day after the Battle of Clontarf. His son, Edmund, died in November 1016 and Edmund's death ensured that Cnut 'succeeded to the whole kingdom of England' in 1017.[30] From this base, Cnut went on to build his Scandinavian empire, taking control in Denmark in 1019, conquering part of Sweden around 1027 and seizing Norway in 1028.[31]

By 1028, Sitric felt secure enough in his power to go on pilgrimage to Rome, along with his neighbour, the king of Brega.[32] The continued great wealth of the town of Dublin after the Battle of Clontarf can be gauged in the entry of AU for the next year, 1029. Sitric's son, Amlaíb, was captured by the new king of Brega, Mathgamain Ua Riacáin. For Amlaíb's ransom, the Hiberno-Norse of Dublin paid Ua Riacáin '1,200 cows and six score

25 *Orkneyinga Saga*, pp 74–5.   26 Holm, 'The slave trade of Dublin', 333; *AFM*, 1018 [*recte* 1019]; *AU*, 1031.   27 *AU*, 1018, 1021; *AFM*, 1021 (note e).   28 Benjamin Hudson, 'Cnut and Viking Dublin' in *Irish Sea studies*, pp 47–59; Clarke, 'Sitriuc Silkbeard', *DIB*, 8, pp 974–7; Campbell (ed.), *Encomium Emmae Reginae*; Valante, *The Vikings in Ireland*, p. 152.   29 *ASC*, 1015, 1016.   30 Ibid., 1016, 1017; Warner (ed. and trans.), *The Chronicon of Thietmar of Merseburg*, 1016, pp 335–6; Lavelle, *Aethelred II*, pp 131–8; Gabriel Ronay, *The lost king of England: the East European adventures of Edward the Exile* (Woodbridge, 2000), pp 3–25.   31 Lawson, *Cnut: England's Viking king*, pp 88–98.   32 *AU*, 1028; King Sitric returned the same year, *AT*, ii, p. 368.

Welsh horses and sixty ounces of gold and the sword of Carlus … and sixty ounces of pure silver'.[33] According to the late medieval Black Book of Christ Church, Sitric Silkenbeard was also responsible for the foundation of Christ Church Cathedral in Dublin at this time. Sitric donated 'a place to build … together with' land, stock and crops, as well as 'gold and silver sufficient to build the church'.[34] Sitric's son Amlaíb was killed in England in 1034 'by the Saxons on his way to Rome', perhaps as he attempted to call at the court of King Cnut.[35] It is probably no coincidence that Sitric himself was deposed as king of Dublin in the months after Cnut's death in 1035.[36] The king of Dublin was a very old man when he was ousted in 1036 by a distant Viking relative from Waterford. Sitric had had Ragnall Ua hÍmair, king of Waterford, killed in Dublin in 1035. It was Ragnall's son Echmarcach who then chased him out of Dublin in 1036. It is stated that he 'went from his realm over the sea' (*Sitriuc mac Amlaim do dul assa righi tar muir*) and died in 1042.[37] Upon his death, AI still referred to Sitric as 'king of Áth Cliath'.[38]

33 *AU*, 1029. **34** *The antiquities and history of Ireland*, p. 65; Gwynn and Hadcock, *Medieval religious houses: Ireland*, p. 70; Aubrey Gwynn, 'Some unpublished texts from the Black Book of Christ Church, Dublin', *Analecta Hibernica*, 16 (1946), 308–9. **35** *AU*, 1034. **36** Ibid., 1035; *ASC*, 1035. **37** *AU*, 1035; *AT*, ii, p. 376; Ailbhe MacShamhráin, 'Echmarcach', *DIB*, 3, p. 571. **38** *AI*, 1042.

Conclusion

The Battle of Clontarf was one of the most remarkable battles in Irish history and it is certainly the most noteworthy of the medieval era. In medieval Irish history, it has no equivalent. In the wider history of these islands, Clontarf must rank with the Battle of Hastings, fought in 1066 between the Anglo-Saxon army of King Harold Godwinson and the invading Norman forces of Duke William the Conqueror.[1] It is also comparable to Bannockburn, fought in 1314 between the army of Robert Bruce (King Robert I), fighting for Scottish independence, against an English army commanded by King Edward II, for its subsequent impact on the history of a people of these islands.[2] While Clontarf may not have been fought to expel the Viking invaders from Ireland, King Brian's career and his seeming ambition for a unified Irish kingdom were remarkable in their own right. The fact that he and his son Murchad died on the battlefield is partly what has given the battle its enduring interest throughout the centuries. Another reason for the continuing fascination with the Battle of Clontarf must lie with the rich saga material relating to the battle that survives in both Irish and Scandinavian traditions.

The impact of the Battle of Clontarf was substantial and it is most clearly seen in the effects that the death of so many leaders from both sides had on the subsequent history of their domains. King Brian's dynasty, the Dál Cais, did not recover its pre-eminent position on the island of Ireland until the period 1072–5, when Brian's grandson, Turlough Ua Briain (son of Tadhg), became the most powerful king on the island.[3] Thus, it took the Dál Cais sixty years to recover from the losses incurred by their ruling dynasty at Clontarf. That it took them so long to recover their power after the death

---

1 *ASC*, 1066; Frank Barlow, *The Godwins* (Harlow, 2002), pp 139–55; ibid., *Edward the Confessor* (London, 1997); ibid. (ed. and trans.), *The Carmen de Hastingae Proelio of Guy Bishop of Amiens* (Oxford, 1999); D.C. Douglas, *William the Conqueror* (London, 1999); Lawson, *The Battle of Hastings, 1066*, pp 199–242; Glyn S. Burgess (ed.), *The history of the Norman people: Wace's Roman de Rou* (Woodbridge, 2004), pp 166–92. 2 Seymour Phillips, *Edward II* (London, 2010), pp 223–37. 3 *AU*, 1072, 1073, 1075.

of Brian in 1014 suggests that the Battle of Clontarf should indeed be viewed as a pyrrhic victory for the Munstermen. Similarly, it took the jarldom of Orkney about thirty years to recover from the death of Jarl Sigurd Hlodvisson at Clontarf. His son, Thorfinn the Mighty, did not begin to rule unchallenged in Orkney until around 1045. The subsequent decline of the jarldom of Orkney after Thorfinn's death around 1058 has been attributed to the lingering effects that the Battle of Clontarf continued to have on Orkney. These were the main obvious implications of the battle.

The Uí Néill lost the high-kingship of Ireland in 1022 on the death of Máelsechnaill II. This cannot be attributed to the effects of the Battle of Clontarf. If anything, the death of Brian and his son Murchad in 1014 provided an excellent opportunity for the Uí Néill to regain and re-impose the traditional high-kingship. It was Brian Boru's successful career before Clontarf that began the process that ended the traditional monarchy of Ireland. As the first non-Uí Néill high-king, Brian challenged whatever legitimacy the Uí Néill high-kingship possessed. The failure of Flaithbertach Ua Néill's bid for the high-kingship in the years after 1022 further damaged this legitimacy. The long interregnum until Brian's grandson, Turlough, became 'king of Ireland' in the 1070s, and the fact that Turlough was not of the Uí Néill, finally finished the old-style high-kingship.[4]

Although the Hiberno-Norse of Dublin had many warriors killed at Clontarf, Sitric Silkenbeard's rule and the wealth of the town continued for many years, unaffected by defeat in 1014. Indeed, Sitric seems to have enjoyed the patronage of King Cnut, the ruler of England and most of Scandinavia, in the years after the Battle of Clontarf. It was only when Diarmait mac Máel na mBó, who was from the south Leinster Uí Cheinnselaig dynasty, seized the kingship of Leinster in 1042 that the era of powerful Irish kings aggressively placing kinsmen in authority over the town of Dublin began.[5] Again, the Battle of Clontarf had little to do with this. It is evident from the Icelandic sagas that Dublin continued to play a

---

4 Ibid., 1086; *AI*, 1086.   **5** Byrne, *Irish kings and high-kings*, pp 271–2.

prominent role in the Scandinavian world. The jarls of Orkney maintained an interest in Ireland after Clontarf.[6] According to Orkneyinga Saga, when Thorfinn the Mighty died around 1058 his court poet Arnor composed a verse to commemorate the jarl's great power, stating that 'the raven-feaster ruled right from Dublin'.[7] Svein Asleifarson, 'a notorious intriguer and violent mercenary' from Orkney, was later active as a Viking raider around Dublin at the time of the fall of the town to the Anglo-Normans.[8] There continued to be kings of Scandinavian descent ruling Dublin until 1170. In that year, the Anglo-Normans captured the town and expelled the Hiberno-Norse from their own settlement.[9]

Therefore, it is the extensive casualty list from the Battle of Clontarf, fought north of Dublin on Good Friday 1014, that had the greatest impact on subsequent Irish history. The same effect of the battle can be observed in the history of the jarldom of Orkney. The main reason for the important place that the Battle of Clontarf holds in Irish history is the fact that King Brian's descendants in the early twelfth century commissioned a saga account of his life and the battle, that has proved to be enduringly popular among the Irish ever since. Similarly, the Hiberno-Norse remained in control of the town of Dublin until 1170, thus ensuring the spread of saga material relating to the Battle of Clontarf in the Scandinavian world. This process was assisted by the fact that Orkney retained its Scandinavian culture throughout the medieval period.[10] In reality, Clontarf was a large, very hard-fought battle, with many prominent casualties and a tragic ending when Brian was killed just as his army was victorious. Nevertheless, it is Brian's career, and the fact that he became the first non-Uí Néill high-king of Ireland, that remain the remarkable and noteworthy parts of his legacy.

---

6 *Orkneyinga Saga*, pp 41, 75.   **7** Ibid., p. 75.   **8** Ibid., pp 214–17; Forte, Oram and Pedersen (eds), *Viking empires*, p. 286.   **9** *AFM*, 1170, 1171.   **10** Bo Almqvist, *Viking ale: studies on folklore contacts between the northern and the western worlds* (Aberystwyth, 1991), pp 1–29.

Postscript

One final link between Scandinavia and the Battle of Clontarf needs to be assessed. This is the career of the later king of Norway, Magnús Barelegs, who took a great interest in Dublin and the Irish Sea region and may have had a substantial if inadvertent influence on the writing of *CGRG*. Magnús, whom the Irish called 'king of Lochlann', was active in the Irish Sea in the years 1098 to 1103.[1] According to the Icelandic saga, Heimskringla or History of the Kings of Norway, written by Snorri Sturluson (d. 1241), Magnús received his nickname Barelegs from a fondness for Irish culture and his adoption of Irish dress. The saga states that when Magnús returned from one of his earlier expeditions 'to the west, he and many of his men for the most part had the manners and wore the clothes which were customary in the British Islands. They went barelegged in the street and had short kirtles and outer garments. Then people called him Magnús Barefoot or Barelegs'.[2] *CGRG* may have been commissioned at this time by Brian's great-grandson, the king of Ireland, Muirchertach Ua Briain, perhaps to inspire his warriors to fight the Norwegians if they attacked his interests in Ireland.[3] Alternatively, the saga may even have been written to entertain King Magnús at the court of Ua Briain, for both Heimskringla and the Irish annals indicate that Muirchertach and Magnús built such a good relationship with each other that, after having 'won much of the land, Dublin and the shire of Dublin', Magnús Barelegs 'in the winter following … dwelt in [Munster] with King Myrjartak, putting his men to the defence of the land he had won'.[4] Although the Norwegians regarded the Irish as 'treacherous', Heimskringla states that Muirchertach Ua Briain 'kept all the

---

1 *AU*, 1098, 1102, 1103; *AI*, 1102, 1103; *ASC*, 1098; E. Curtis, 'Murchertach O'Brien, high-king of Ireland, and his Norman son-in-law, Arnulf De Montgomery', *JRSAI*, 11:2 (1921), 116–24. **2** *Heimskringla*, p. 681. **3** Máire Ní Mhaonaigh has suggested a date of composition between the years 1103 and 1113: Máire Ní Mhaonaigh, 'The date of Cogad Gáedel re Gallaib', *Peritia*, 9 (1995), 354–77; A.J. Goedheer went for a slightly later date, 1132–5: Goedheer, *Irish and Norse traditions about the Battle of Clontarf*, p. 10. **4** *Heimskringla*, pp 683–4; *AI*, 1102; *AU*, 1102.

promises he had made to King Magnús'.[5] King Magnús Barelegs was killed in 1103, 'when taken unawares by the Ulaid'.[6] Heimskringla records that Magnús was killed after landing on the coast of Ulster to collect supplies sent by Muirchertach Ua Briain, having been ambushed in a wooded pass over a bog by the Ulaid on his return to his ships. Magnús 'was wounded by a spear passing through both his thighs above the knee', and killed when he 'received a blow with a battle-axe on his neck, and that was his death wound'.[7] With the death of Magnús Barelegs, Cogagh Gaedhel re Gallaibh may have served its purpose (whatever it was), by assisting Muirchertach Ua Briain against this Norwegian king in the Irish Sea region.

5 *Heimskringla*, pp 684–5.   6 *AI*, 1103; *AU*, 1103.   7 *Heimskringla*, pp 684–7.

Appendix 1: The Battle of Maldon (AD991)

The following extracts are taken from an account of the Battle of Maldon, fought on the coast of Essex between the Anglo-Saxon army of Ealdorman Byrhtnoth and the Scandinavian force of Olaf Tryggvason on either 10 or 11 August 991.[1] This contemporary information on the battle is preserved in some rare Anglo-Saxon poetry. The original manuscript was destroyed in a fire in 1731.[2]

> Then he commanded each one of the soldiers to set his horse loose, to drive it far away and to proceed on foot, and to turn his mind to his hands and a doughty disposition …
>
> Then Byrhtnoth began to place the men in array there; he rode about and gave instructions, taught the soldiers how they were to stand and maintain the position and urged them that they should hold their shields properly, securely with their fists, and that they should not feel scared at all. When he had suitably placed the army in array he then dismounted among the people where it pleased him best to be, where he knew his troop of household retainers to be most loyal.
>
> 'Do you hear, sea-wanderer, what this nation says? They will give you spears as tribute, the poison-tipped javelin and ancient swords, those warlike accoutrements which will profit you nothing in battle. Seamen's spokesman, report back again; tell your people much more distasteful news: that here stands a worthy earl with his troop of men who is willing to defend this his ancestral home, the country of Æthelred, my lord's nation and land … '

1 *ASC*, 991.　2 Bradley, *Anglo-Saxon poetry*, pp 518–28.

Then the lord of the English heroes commanded a warrior hardy in war to hold the causeway – he was called Wulfstan, a man valiant by virtue of his family. He was son of Ceola who with his spear fatally shot the first man who very rashly stepped on to the causeway there. ...

The slaughterous wolves advanced; they gave no heed to the water, that troop of Vikings. Westwards across the Pante, across the gleaming water they carried their shields; the men from the fleet bore their linden targes ashore. There, confronting the fierce foe, Byrhtnoth stood ready with his men. He ordered the army to form the defensive barrier with shields and to hold steadfastly against their enemies.

Then from their fists they let fly spears hard as a file, cruelly sharpened javelins. Bows were busy, shield caught point. The onslaught was furious. Warriors fell, soldiers lay dead on either side. Wulfmaer was wounded. He had chosen death in battle this relative of Byrhtnoth, son of his sister: he was violently hacked down by swords. Retribution was paid to the Vikings for that. I heard that Eadweard violently struck one with his sword – he did not skimp the blow – so that the doomed fighter fell dead at his feet; for this his lord declared his thanks to the chamberlain when he had the chance.

Then one of the Viking warriors let go a spear from his hands, let it fly from his fist so that it went all too deeply into Æthelred's noble thane. By his side a youth not grown to manhood was standing, a boy in the battle, who very bravely plucked the spear out of the man, the son of Wulfstan, young Wulfmaer. He made the extremely hard spear return again. The point penetrated so that he who had just now severely struck his lord lay dead on the ground.

Then an armed fellow went towards the earl – he wanted to take the man's valuables, his armour and rings and ornamented sword. Then Byrhtnoth drew sword from sheath, broad and bright of blade, and struck against the corslet. All too quickly one of the shipmen hindered him, since he crippled the earl's arm. The golden hilted sword then fell to the earth: he was unable to hold the hard blade, or wield a weapon. Even then, the grey-haired warrior delivered a harangue, emboldened the young men and urged them to press onwards as good comrades. Then he was unable to stand steadily on his feet any longer. He looked up to the heavens.

Then heathen warriors hacked him down, and both the men who were standing by him, Ælfnoth and Wulmaer both lay dead, who gave their lives at the side of their lord.

Then those who had no will to stay there made off from the conflict. The sons of Odda first took flight there; Godric took flight from the battle and deserted the good man who had often given him many a horse. He leapt on to the mount which belonged to his lord, into those trappings, as it was not proper for him to do, and both his brothers ran away with him, Godwine and Godwig: they had no taste for fighting, but turned away from the battle and made for the forest; they fled into that secure place and saved their lives – and more men than it was in any way fitting, if they had called to mind all the favours which Byrhtnoth had done for their benefit.

So the leader of that people was laid low in death. Those of his personal retinue all saw that their lord lay dead. Then, proud thanes, they went on forwards; eagerly they pressed on, men without fear. At that point they all desired one of two things – to render up their life or to avenge the man they had loved.

Appendix 2: The death of King Brian as recounted in Cogadh Gaedhel re Gallaibh

His cushion was readjusted under Brian and he sang fifty psalms, and fifty prayers, and fifty paters; and the fighting continued all that time. He asked then of the attendant, in what state were the forces? The attendant answered: 'They appear to me the same as if Tomar's Wood was on fire, and the seven battalions had been cutting away its underwood and its young shoots, for a month, leaving its stately trees and its immense oaks standing. In such manner are the armies on either side, after the greater part of them have fallen, leaving a few brave men and gallant heroes only standing … and the foreigners are now defeated, and Murchad's standard has fallen'.[1] 'That is sad news', said Brian … 'Woe is me', said the attendant, 'if thou wouldst take my advice, thou wouldst mount thy horse, and we would go to the camp, and remain there amongst the servants; and everyone who escapes this battle will come unto us, and around us will they all rally.[2] Besides, the battalions are now mixed together in confusion; and a party of the foreigners have rejected the idea of retreating to the sea; and we know not who may approach us where we now are'. 'Oh God! Thou boy', said Brian, 'retreat becomes us not, and I myself know that I shall not leave this place alive; and what would it profit me if I did?' …

While they were engaged in this conversation, the attendant perceived a party of the foreigners approaching them. The Jarl Brodir was there, and two warriors along with him. 'There are people coming towards us here', said the attendant. 'Woe is me, what manner of people are they?' asked Brian. 'A blue stark naked people', said the attendant. 'Alas!', said Brian, 'they are the foreigners of the armour, and it is not to do good to thee they

---

1 The Cogadh records the name of Brian's servant as 'Latean from whom are the O'Lateans, still in Munster': *CGRG*, pp 196–7 (note 2). 2 According to the Annals of the Four Masters, the Cenél nEógain high-king Niall Glúndub requested 'a horse to carry him from the battle' at Dublin in 919 from his confessor (*anmchara*) Celedabhaill, who refused him, and Niall was killed as a result, *AFM*, 917 [*recte* 919].

come'. While he was saying this, he arose and stepped off the cushion, and unsheathed his sword. Brodir passed him by and noticed him not. One of the three who were there, and who had been in Brian's service said 'King, King', said he, 'this is the king'. 'No, no, but Priest, Priest', said Brodir, 'it is not he', says he, 'but a noble priest'. 'By no means', said the soldier, 'that is the great king, Brian'. Brodir then turned round, and appeared with a bright, gleaming, trusty battle-axe in his hand, with the handle set in the middle of it. When Brian saw him he gazed at him, and gave him a stroke with his sword, and cut off his left leg at the knee, and his right leg at the foot. The foreigner dealt Brian a stroke which cleft his head utterly; and Brian killed the second man that was with Brodir, and they fell mutually by each other.[3]

3 *CGRG*, pp 198–203.

Appendix 3: The death of King Brian according to Njal's Saga

As for King Brian, he did not want to fight on Friday, and so a shieldburg was thrown up around him and the army was drawn up in front of him …

The ranks went at each other. The fighting was very fierce. Brodir went through the enemy force and killed everybody who was in his way, and no steel could bite him. But then Ulf Hraeda came up against him and thrust at him three times so hard that Brodir fell down each time and could scarcely get back on his feet.[1] When he finally picked himself up he fled into the woods …

Brodir saw that King Brian's forces were chasing the fugitives and that there were only a few men at the shieldburg. He ran out of the woods and cut his way through the shieldburg and swung at the king. The boy Tadhg brought his arm up against it, but the blow cut off the arm and the king's head too, and the king's blood fell on the stump of the boy's arm, and the stump healed at once.[2]

Then Brodir called loudly, 'Let word go from man to man – Brodir killed Brian'.[3]

---

[1] It has been suggested that the character Ulf Hraeda is an attempt by the author of Njal's Saga to render the name of Brian's bodyguard Cúduiligh into Old Norse: Ní Mhaonaigh, *Brian Boru*, pp 89–90. Cúduiligh, however, was a grandnephew of Brian (the son of Cennétig son of Brian's brother Donncuan), rather than a brother of the high-king himself as related in the saga. In fact, there is no brother of Brian Boru called Cúduiligh recorded in the Dál Cais genealogies, and if he did exist he could have been no younger than 63 in 1014, much too old to have been an effective bodyguard. Cúduiligh being Brian's grandnephew was probably around thirty years of age in 1014. As a result, any link with Ulf Hraeda, who is probably a figment of the saga-writer's imagination, is very tenuous. I believe that it is a mistake to try to find a historical basis for much of what appears in the Irish and Icelandic sagas. **2** According to this saga, 'the boy Tadhg' was Brian's younger son. I have never seen it recorded anywhere else that Tadhg was maimed at Clontarf defending his father. Tadhg, son of Brian, was also an adult by 1014. **3** *Njal's Saga*, pp 301–3.

A STANZA OF SCANDINAVIAN POETRY FROM NJAL'S SAGA

When swords screamed in Ireland
and men struggled, I was there;
many a weapon was shattered
when shields met in battle.
The attack, I hear was daring;
Sigurd died in the din of helmets
after making bloody wounds;
Brian fell too, but won.[4]

THE LAST TWO LINES AS GIVEN IN GEORGE DASENT'S
MORE OLD FASHIONED TRANSLATION OF 1861

Brian fell, but kept his kingdom
Ere he lost one drop of blood.[5]

4 Ibid., pp 307–8.   5 Dasent (ed.), *The story of burnt Njal*, ii, p. 343.

Bibliography

MANUSCRIPTS

Germany
Bayerische Staatsbibliotek, München
Sacramentary of Emperor Henry II, Clm 4456

Ireland
National Library of Ireland, Dublin (NLI)
MS 21F51: The Longfield Map Collection
Trinity College Dublin (TCD)
MS 52: The Book of Armagh
MS 58: The Book of Kells

United Kingdom
British Museum (BM)
MS Egerton 90, Fragment of the Book of Uí Mhaine: poem relating to Tadhg
   Ua Ceallaigh and the Clann Ceallaigh
National Maritime Museum, Greenwich (NMM)
MS 16P/49(10) Map of Dublin Bay (1673)

PRINTED PRIMARY SOURCES

Barlow, Frank (ed.), *The Carmen de Hastingae Proelio of Guy, bishop of Amiens*
   (Oxford, 1999).
Barlow, Frank (ed.), *The life of King Edward who rests at Westminster* (Oxford,
   1992).
Best, R.I., and Osborn Bergin, Lebor na hUidre: *Book of the Dun Cow* (Dublin,
   1929).
Binchy, D.A., *Corpus Iuris Hibernici*, 3 (Dublin, 1978).
Bourgain, P. (ed.), 'Ademari Cabannensis Chronicon', *Corpus Christianorum:*
   continuation mediaevalis, 129 (Turnhout, 1999).
Bradley, S.A.J. (ed.), *Anglo-Saxon poetry* (London, 1995).
Broderick, George (ed.), Chronica regum manniae et insularum: *Chronicles of*
   the kings of Man and the Isles (Douglas, 2004).
Bugge, Alexander (ed.), Caithreim Cellachain Caisil: *the victorious career of*

133

Cellachan of Cashel or the wars between the Irishmen and the Norsemen in the middle of the 10th century (Christiania, 1905).

Burgess, Glyn S. (ed.), *The history of the Norman people Wace's Roman de Rou* (Woodbridge, 2004).

Burgess, Glyn S. (ed.), *The Song of Roland* (London, 1990).

Cook, Robert, *Njal's Saga* (London, 2001).

Foote, P.G. (ed.), and R. Quirk (trans.), *The saga of Gunnlaug Serpent-Tongue* (London, 1957).

Gleeson, D., 'The Annals of Nenagh', *Analecta Hibernica*, 12 (1943), 155–64.

Gleeson, D., and Seán MacAirt, 'The Annals of Roscrea', *PRIA*, 59C3 (1958), 137–80.

Gwynn, Aubrey, 'Some unpublished texts from the Black Book of Christ Church, Dublin', *Analecta Hibernica*, 16 (1946), 281–338.

Gwynn, Edward (ed.), *The metrical Dindsenchas, part I: text, translation and commentary: Todd Lecture Series*, 8 (Dublin, 1903).

Gwynn, John (ed.), Liber Ardmachanus: *The Book of Armagh* (Dublin, 1913).

Hayes O'Grady, Standish (ed.), Caithréim Thoirdhealbhaigh: *The Triumphs of Turlough, by Sean (Mac Ruaidhrí) Mac Craith*, 1 & 2 (London, 1929).

Hennessy, William (ed.), *Chronicon Scotorum: a chronicle of Irish affairs from the earliest times to AD1135, with a supplement containing the events from 1141 to 1150* (London, 1866).

Hennessy, William (ed.), *The Annals of Loch Cé: a chronicle of Irish affairs from AD1014 to AD1590*, 1 (London, 1871).

Henthorn Todd, James (ed.), Cogadh Gaedhel re Gallaibh: *War of the Gaedhil with the Gaill* (London, 1867).

Hollander, Lee M. (ed.), *Heimskringla: history of the kings of Norway* (Austin, 2007).

Jones, Thomas (ed.), Brut Y Tywysogyon *or The Chronicle of the Princes: Peniarth MS 20 version* (Cardiff, 1952).

Keynes, Simon, and Alistair Campbell (eds), Encomium Emmae Reginae (Cambridge, 1998).

Mac Airt, Seán (ed.), *The Annals of Inisfallen* (Dublin, 1988).

Mac Airt, Seán, and Gearóid Mac Niocaill (eds), *The Annals of Ulster (to AD1131)* (Dublin, 2004).

Macalister, R.A.S. (ed.), *Lebor Gabála Erenn: the book of the taking of Ireland* (Dublin, 1956).

Magnusson, Magnus and Hermann Pálsson (eds), *King Harald's Saga* (London, 2005).

Murphy, Denis (ed.), *The Annals of Clonmacnoise being Annals of Ireland from the earliest period to AD1408, translated into English AD1627 by Conell Mageoghagan* (Dublin, 1896).

Murray, Kevin (ed.), Baile in Scáil, *'The Phantom's Frenzy'* (Dublin, 2004).

Ní Úrdail, Meidhbhín (ed.), Cath Cluana Tarbh, '*The Battle of Clontarf*' (Dublin, 2011).

O'Brien, M.A. (ed.), Corpus Genealogiarum Hiberniae (Dublin, 1962).

O'Donovan, John (ed.), *Annals of the Kingdom of Ireland by the Four Masters* (Dublin, 1856).

O'Donovan, John (ed.), *The Circuit of Ireland by Muircheartach MacNeill, prince of Aileach: a poem written in the year 942 by Cormacan Eigeas, chief poet of the north of Ireland* (Dublin, 1841).

Ó Muráile, Nollaig (ed.), Leabhar Mór Na nGenealach: *the great book of Irish genealogies* (Dublin, 2003).

O'Sullivan, Anne (ed.), *The Book of Leinster formerly* Lebor na Núachongbála, 6 (Dublin, 1983).

O'Sullivan, Denis C. (ed.), *The natural history of Ireland by Philip O'Sullivan Beare* (Cork, 2009).

Pálsson, Hermann, and Paul Edwards (eds), *Orkneyinga Saga: the history of the earls of Orkney* (London, 1981).

Scott, A.B., and F.X. Martin (eds), Expugnatio Hibernica: *The conquest of Ireland, by Giraldus Cambrensis* (Dublin, 1978).

Swanton, Michael (ed.), *The Anglo-Saxon Chronicles* (London, 2000).

Stokes, Whitley (trans.), *The Annals of Tigernach* (repr. from *Revue Celtique* (1895/6) (Felinfach, 1993).

Vries, Ranke de (ed.), *Two texts on Lough Neagh:* De causis torchi Corc' Óche *and* Aided Echach maic Maireda (Dublin, 2012).

Waitz, Georg (ed.), '*Mariani Scotti Chronicon*' in George Pertz (ed.), *Monumenta Germaniae Historica*, 5 (Hanover, 1844; www.mgh.de).

Warner, David A. (ed.), *Ottonian Germany: the Chronicon of Thietmar of Merseburg* (Manchester, 2001).

Webbe Dasent, George (ed.), *The story of Burnt Njal* (Edinburgh, 1861).

Whitelock, Dorothy (ed.), Sermo Lupi Ad Anglos (Exeter, 1989).

Williams, N.J.A. (ed.), *The poems of Giolla Brighde Mac Con Midhe* (Dublin, 1980).

SECONDARY SOURCES

Abrams, Lesley, 'The conversion of the Scandinavians of Dublin', *Anglo-Norman Studies*, 20 (Woodbridge, 1998), 1–30.

Almqvist, Bo, and Dáithí Ó hÓgáin, Skálda: éigse is eachtraíocht sa tSean-Lochlainn (Baile Átha Cliath, 1995).

Almqvist, Bo, *Viking ale: studies on folklore contacts between the northern and western worlds* (Aberystwyth, 1991).

Andrew McDonald, R., *Manx kingship in its Irish Sea setting, 1187–1229: King Rǫgnvaldr and the Crovan dynasty* (Dublin, 2007).

Andrews, J.H., 'The oldest map of Dublin', *PRIA*, 83C7 (1983), 205–37.

Barlow, Frank, *Edward the Confessor* (London, 1997).

Barlow, Frank, *The Godwins: the rise and fall of a noble dynasty* (Harlow, 2003).

Barraclough, Geoffrey, *The Times atlas of world history: revised edition* (London, 1986).

Bartlett, Thomas, and Keith Jeffery (eds), *A military history of Ireland* (Cambridge, 1996).

Bowlus, Charles R., *The Battle of Lechfeld and its aftermath, August 955* (Aldershot, 2006).

Bradbury, Jim, *The Routledge companion to medieval warfare* (London, 2004).

Bradley, John (ed.), *Settlement and society in medieval Ireland: studies presented to F.X. Martin* (Kilkenny, 1988).

Bradley, John, 'Killaloe: a pre-Norman borough', *Peritia*, 8 (1994), 170–9.

Bradley, John, 'Some reflections on the problem of Scandinavian settlement in the hinterland of Dublin during the ninth century' in Bradley et al. (eds), *Dublin in the medieval world*, pp 39–62.

Bradley, John, 'The interpretation of Scandinavian settlement in Ireland' in Bradley (ed.), *Settlement and society*, pp 49–78.

Bradley, John, Alan J. Fletcher and Anngret Simms (eds), *Dublin in the medieval world: studies in honour of Howard B. Clarke* (Dublin, 2009).

Bradley, John, and Andrew Halpin, 'The topographical development of Scandinavian and Anglo-Norman Cork' in P. O'Flanagan and C. Buttimer (eds), *Cork: history and society* (Dublin, 1993), pp 15–44.

Byrne, Francis J., *Irish kings and high-kings* (London, 1987).

Byrne, Francis J., *The rise of the Uí Néill and the high-kingship of Ireland: O'Donnell Lecture* (Dublin, 1969).

Campbell, James, *The Anglo-Saxons* (London, 1991).

Charles-Edwards, T.M., 'Irish warfare before 1100' in Bartlett and Jeffery (eds), *A military history of Ireland*, pp 26–51.

Christiansen, Reidar Th., *The Vikings and the Viking wars in Irish and Gaelic tradition* (Oslo, 1931).

Clarke, Howard B., 'From Dyflinnarskíri to the Pale: defining and defending a medieval city-state, 1000–1500' in Ní Ghrádaigh and O'Byrne (eds), *The March in the islands of the medieval West*, pp 35–52.

Clarke, Howard B., 'Unsung heroes: the Irish and the Viking wars' in Sheehan and Ó Corráin (eds), *The Viking Age: Ireland and the West*, pp 60–5.

Clinton, Mark, 'Settlement patterns in the early historic kingdom of Leinster' in Smyth (ed.), *Seanchas*, pp 275–98.

Curtis, Edmund, 'Murchertach O'Brien, high-king of Ireland, and his Norman son-in-law, Arnulf de Montgomery, *circa* 1100', *JRSAI*, sixth ser., 11:2 (1921), 116–24.

Dillon, Charles, and Henry A. Jefferies (eds), *Tyrone: history and society* (Dublin, 2000).

Doherty, Charles, Linda Doran and Mary Kelly (eds), *Glendalough: City of God* (Dublin, 2011).

Dolley, Michael, 'Some Irish evidence for the date of the *Crux* coins of Æthelred II', *Anglo-Saxon England*, 2 (Cambridge, 1973), 145–54.

Douglas, David C., *William the Conqueror* (London, 1999).

Downham, Claire, 'Religious and cultural boundaries between Vikings and Irish: the evidence of conversion' in Ní Ghrádaigh and O'Byrne (eds), *The March in the islands of the medieval West*, pp 15–34.

Downham, Claire, 'The Vikings in Southern Uí Néill until 1014', *Peritia*, 17–18 (2003–4), 233–55.

Downham, Claire, *Viking Kings of Britain and Ireland: the dynasty of Ívarr to AD1014* (Edinburgh, 2007).

Duffy, Seán (ed.), *Medieval Ireland: an encyclopedia* (New York, 2005).

Duffy, Seán, 'Ireland and Scotland, 1014–1169: contacts and caveats' in Smyth (ed.), *Seanchas*, pp 348–56.

Duffy, Seán, 'Irishmen and Islesmen in the kingdoms of Dublin and Man, 1052–1171', *Ériu*, 43 (1992), 93–133.

Enright, Michael J., *Lady with a mead cup: ritual, prophecy and lordship in the European warband from La Tène to the Viking Age* (Dublin, 1996).

Eogan, George, 'Life and living at Lagore' in Smyth (ed.), *Seanchas*, pp 64–82.

Etchingham, Colmán, 'Evidence of Scandinavian settlement in Wicklow' in Ken Hannigan and William Nolan (eds), *Wicklow: history and society* (Dublin, 1994), pp 113–38.

Etchingham, Colmán, 'The organization and function of an early Irish church settlement: what was Glendalough?' in Doherty et al. (eds), *Glendalough: City of God*, pp 22–53.

Etchingham, Colmán, 'The Viking impact on Glendalough' in Doherty et al. (eds), *Glendalough: City of God*, pp 211–22.

Fanning, Thomas, 'Three ringed pins from Viking Dublin and their significance' in Bradley (ed.), *Settlement and society*, pp 161–76.

Flanagan, Deirdre, 'Cráeb Telcha: Crew. Co. Antrim', *Dinnseanchas*, 4:2 (1970), 29–32.

Flanagan, Marie Therese, 'Irish and Anglo-Norman warfare in twelfth-century Ireland' in Bartlett and Jeffery (eds), *A military history of Ireland*, pp 52–75.

Foot, Sarah, *Æthelstan: the first king of England* (London, 2011).

Forte, Angelo, Richard Oram and Frederik Pedersen, *Viking empires* (Cambridge, 2005).

Foster, R.F. (ed.), *The Oxford illustrated history of Ireland* (Oxford, 1991).

Garrison, Eliza, *Ottonian imperial art: the artistic patronage of Otto III and Henry II* (Farnham, 2012).

Goedheer, A.J., *Irish and Norse traditions about the Battle of Clontarf* (Haarlem, 1938).

Gray, James, *Sutherland and Caithness in saga-time* (London, 1922).

Grogan, Eoin, and Annaba Kilfeather, *Archaeological inventory of County Wicklow* (Dublin, 1997).

Gwynn, Aubrey, 'Brian in Armagh (1005)', *Seanchas Ard Macha*, 9:1 (1978), 35–50.

Gwynn, Aubrey, and R.N. Hadcock (eds), *Medieval religious houses: Ireland* (Dublin, 1988).

Halpin, Andrew, 'Weapons and warfare in Viking-Age Ireland' in Sheehan and Ó Corráin (eds), *The Viking Age: Ireland and the West*, pp 124–35.

Halpin, Andrew, *Weapons and warfare in Viking and medieval Dublin* (Dublin, 2008).

Hamlin, Ann, 'The early church in Tyrone to the twelfth-century' in Dillon and Jefferies (eds), *Tyrone: history and society*, pp 85–126.

Harney, Lorcan, 'Medieval burial and pilgrimage within the landscape of Glendalough: the evidence of the crosses and cross-slabs' in Doherty et al. (eds), *Glendalough: City of God*, pp 112–36.

Haughton, Samuel, and James Henthorn Todd, *The tides of Dublin Bay and the Battle of Clontarf, 23rd April, 1014* (Dublin, 1861).

Haworth, Richard, 'The site of St Olave's Church, Dublin' in Bradley (ed.), *Settlement and society*, pp 177–91.

Hayes-McCoy, G.A., *Irish battles: a military history of Ireland* (Belfast, 1990).

Hickey, Kieran, *Wolves in Ireland: a natural and cultural history* (Dublin, 2011).

Hogan, J., 'The Irish law of kingship, with special reference to Ailech and Cenél Eoghain', *PRIA*, 40C (1931–2), 186–254.

Holm, Poul, 'The slave trade of Dublin, ninth to twelfth centuries', *Peritia*, 5 (1986), 317–45.

Hudson, Benjamin, 'Brjáns Saga', *Medium Ævum*, 71 (2002), 241–68.

Hudson, Benjamin, 'Cnut and Viking Dublin' in Hudson (ed.), *Irish Sea studies*, pp 47–59.

Hudson, Benjamin, 'The changing economy of the Irish Sea province, 900–1300' in Hudson (ed.), *Irish Sea studies*, pp 21–46.

Hudson, Benjamin, *Irish Sea studies, 900–1200* (Dublin, 2006).

Hudson, Benjamin, *Prophecy of Berchán: Irish and Scottish high-kings of the early Middle Ages* (Westport/CT, 1996).

Jesch, Judith, 'The warrior ideal in the late Viking Age' in Sheehan and Ó Corráin (eds), *The Viking Age: Ireland and the West*, pp 165–73.

Kavanagh, Rhoda, 'The horse in Viking Ireland: some observations' in Bradley (ed.), *Settlement and society*, pp 89–122.

Kazhdan, Alexander P. (ed.), *The Oxford dictionary of Byzantium* (Oxford, 1991).

Kelly, E., and E. O'Donovan, 'A Viking longphort near Athlunkard, Co. Clare', *Archaeology Ireland*, 12:4/43 (1998), 13–16.

Kissane, Noel, *Historic Dublin maps* (Dublin, 1988).

Lacey, Brian, 'Monster and monastery? St Kevin's Lives and the expansion of Glendalough' in Doherty et al. (eds), *Glendalough: City of God*, pp 165–74.

Lacey, Brian, *Lug's forgotten Donegal kingdom: the archaeology, history and folklore of the Síl Lugdach of Cloghaneely* (Dublin, 2012).

Lalor, Brian (ed.), *The encyclopaedia of Ireland* (Dublin, 2003).

Lamb, Raymond, 'Kirkwall revisited' in Sheehan and Ó Corráin (eds), *The Viking Age: Ireland and the West*, pp 199–203.

Lane, Alan M., 'Viking-Age and Norse pottery in the Hebrides' in Sheehan and Ó Corráin (eds), *The Viking Age: Ireland and the West*, pp 204–16.

Lavelle, Ryan, *Aethelred II: king of the English, 978–1016* (Stroud, 2004).

Lawson, M.K., *Cnut: England's Viking king, 1016–35* (Stroud, 2011).

Lawson, M.K., *The Battle of Hastings, 1066* (Stroud, 2007).

Leask, H.G., and R.A.S. Macalister, 'Liathmore-Mochoemóg (Leigh), County Tipperary', *PRIA*, 51C1 (1946), 1–14.

Lewis, Samuel, *A topographical dictionary of Ireland*, 1 (London, 1837).

Lucas, A.T., 'The sacred trees of Ireland', *JCHAS*, 68:207/8 (1963), 16–54.

Lucas, A.T., *Treasures of Ireland: Irish, pagan and early Christian art* (Dublin, 1973).

Lund, Niels, 'The armies of Swein Forkbeard and Cnut: *leding* or *lið*?', *Anglo-Saxon England*, 15 (Cambridge, 1986), 105–18.

Mac Niocaill, Gearóid, *Ireland before the Vikings* (Dublin, 1972).

MacCarthy, B., *The Codex Palatino-Vaticanus no. 830: Todd Lecture Series*, 3 (Dublin, 1892).

MacShamhráin, Ailbhe, 'Brian Bóruma, Armagh and high-kingship', *Seanchas Ard Macha*, 20:2 (2005), 1–21.

MacShamhráin, Ailbhe, 'The Battle of Glen Máma, Dublin, and the high-kingship of Ireland: a millennial commemoration' in Seán Duffy (ed.), *Medieval Dublin*, 2 (Dublin, 2001), pp 53–64.

MacShamhráin, Ailbhe, 'The making of Tír nÉogain: Cenél nÉogain and the Airgialla from the sixth to the eleventh centuries' in Dillon and Jefferies (eds), *Tyrone: history and society*, pp 55–84.

Maddox, Melanie C., 'Finding the city of God in the Lives of St Kevin: Glendalough and the history of the Irish celestial civitas' in Doherty et al. (eds), *Glendalough: City of God*, pp 1–21.

Magh Adhair: a ritual and inauguration complex in south-east Clare (Archaeology Ireland Heritage Guide No. 2).

Marsden, John, *Kings, Mormaers, rebels: early Scotland's other royal family* (Edinburgh, 2010).

McGuire, James, and James Quinn (eds), *Dictionary of Irish biography: from the earliest times to the year 2002* (Cambridge, 2009).

McKitterick, Rosamond, *Charlemagne: the formation of a European identity* (Cambridge, 2008).

Meehan, Bernard, *The Book of Kells: an illustrated introduction to the manuscript in Trinity College Dublin* (London, 1994).

Michelli, Perette, 'The inscriptions on pre-Norman Irish reliquaries', *PRIA*, 96CI (1996), 1–48.

Monk, M., and J. Sheehan (eds), *Early medieval Munster: archaeology, history and society* (Cork, 1998).

Ní Dhonnchadha, Máirín, 'On Gormfhlaith daughter of Flann Sinna and the lure of the sovereignty goddess' in Smyth (ed.), *Seanchas*, pp 225–37.

Ní Ghrádaigh, Jenifer, and Emmett O'Byrne (eds), *The March in the islands of the medieval West* (Leiden, 2012).

Ní Mhaonaigh, Máire, 'Cogad Gáedel re Gallaib and the annals: a comparison', *Ériu*, 47 (1996), 101–26.

Ní Mhaonaigh, Máire, 'The date of Cogad Gáedel re Gallaib', *Peritia*, 9 (1995), 354–77.

Ní Mhaonaigh, Máire, '"Celtic and Anglo-Saxon kingship" revisited: Alfred, Æthelred II and Brian Bórama compared' in Bradley et al. (eds), *Dublin in the medieval world*, pp 83–97.

Ní Mhaonaigh, Máire, *Brian Boru: Ireland's greatest king?* (Stroud, 2007).

Ó Carragáin, Tomás, *Churches in early medieval Ireland* (London, 2010).

Ó Corráin, Donncha, '*Caithréim Chellacháin Chaisil*: history or propaganda', *Ériu*, 25 (1974), 1–70.

Ó Corráin, Donncha, 'Muirchertach Mac Lochlainn and the circuit of Ireland' in Smyth (ed.), *Seanchas*, pp 238–50.

Ó Corráin, Donncha, 'Old Norse and medieval Irish: bilingualism in Viking-Age Dublin' in Bradley et al. (eds), *Dublin in the medieval world*, pp 63–72.

Ó Corráin, Donncha, *Ireland before the Normans* (Dublin, 1972).

Ó Cuív, Brian, 'Personal names as an indicator of relations between native Irish and settlers in the Viking period' in Bradley (ed.), *Settlement and society*, pp 79–88.

O'Donoghue, Tadhg, 'Cert cech ríg co réil' in Osborn Bergin and Carl Marstrander (eds), *Miscellany presented to Kuno Meyer* (Halle, 1912).

O'Donovan, John, *The genealogies, tribes and customs of Hy-Fiachrach* (Dublin, 1844).

O'Donovan, John, *The tribes and customs of Hy-Many commonly called O'Kelly's Country* (Dublin, 1843).

O'Gorman, Thomas, 'On the site of the Battle of Clontarf', *JRSAI*, 5:40 (1879), 169–82.

Ó hÓgáin, Dáithí, *Myth, legend & romance: an encyclopædia of the Irish folk tradition* (London, 1990).

Ó Muirithe, Diarmaid, *From the Viking word-hoard: a dictionary of Scandinavian words in the languages of Britain and Ireland* (Dublin, 2010).

O'Neill, Timothy, *The Irish hand: scribes and their manuscripts from the earliest times to the seventeenth century with an exemplar of scripts* (Portlaoise, 1984).

Ó Riain, Diarmuid, 'A Glendalough bishop in Germany? The Four Masters and the three Gilla na Náems' in Doherty et al. (eds), *Glendalough: City of God*, pp 177–82.

Ó Riain, Pádraig, 'The shrine of the Stowe Missal, re-dated', *PRIA*, 91C10 (1991), 285–95.

Ó Riain, Pádraig, *A dictionary of Irish saints* (Dublin, 2011).

Ó Riain-Raedel, Dagmar, 'German influence on Munster church and kings in the twelfth century' in Smyth (ed.), *Seanchas*, pp 323–30.

Phillips, Seymour, *Edward II* (London, 2010).

Picard, Jean-Michel, 'Space organization in early Irish monasteries: the platea' in Doherty et al. (eds), *Glendalough: City of God*, pp 54–63.

Poole, Russell (ed.), *Skaldsagas: text, vocation and desire in the Icelandic Sagas of Poets* (New York, 2001).

Roesdahl, Else, *The Vikings* (London, 1998).

Ronay, Gabriel, *The lost king of England: the east European adventures of Edward the Exile* (Woodbridge, 2000).

Ryan, John, 'Brian Boruma, king of Ireland' in Etienne Rynne (ed.), *North Munster studies* (Limerick, 1967), pp 355–74.

Ryan, John, 'The Battle of Clontarf', *JRSAI*, 68:1 (1938), 1–50.

Ryan, John, 'The Dalcassians', *North Munster Antiquarian Journal*, 3:4 (1943), 191–202.

Rynne, Etienne, 'An Irish sword of the 11th century?', *JRSAI*, 92:2 (1962), 208–10.

Sawyer, Peter, *The Oxford illustrated history of the Vikings* (Oxford, 2001).

Scott, Ian G., and Anna Ritchie, *Pictish and Viking-Age carvings from Shetland* (Edinburgh, 2009).

Sheehan, J., and Donncha Ó Corráin (eds), *The Viking Age: Ireland and the West* (Dublin, 2010).

Simms, Katharine, *From kings to warlords: the changing political structure of Gaelic Ireland in the later Middle Ages* (Woodbridge, 1987).

Smyth, Alfred P. (ed.), *Seanchas: studies in early and medieval Irish archaeology, history and literature in honour of Francis J. Byrne* (Dublin, 2000).

Stenton, Frank, *Anglo-Saxon England* (Oxford, 2001).

Stephenson, Paul, *The legend of Basil the Bulgar-Slayer* (Cambridge, 2003).

Stout, Matthew, *The Irish ringfort* (Dublin, 2000).

The antiquities and history of Ireland by the right honourable Sir James Ware knt (London, 1705).

The Viking Ship Museum, *Welcome on board! The Sea Stallion from Glendalough: a Viking longship recreated* (Roskilde, 2007).

Thornton, David E., 'Clann Eruilb: Irish or Scandinavian?', *IHS*, 30:118 (1996), 161–6.

Tierney, John, 'Wood and woodlands in early medieval Munster' in Monk and Sheehan (eds), *Early medieval Munster*, pp 53–8.

Valante, Mary, 'Viking kings and Irish fleets during Dublin's Viking Age' in Bradley et al. (eds), *Dublin in the medieval world*, pp 73–82.

Valante, Mary, *The Vikings in Ireland: settlement, trade and urbanization* (Dublin, 2008).

Vucinich, Wayne S., and Thomas A. Emmert (eds), *Kosovo: legacy of a medieval battle* (Minneapolis, 1991).

Wallace, P.F., 'Archaeology and the emergence of Dublin as the principal town in Ireland' in Bradley (ed.), *Settlement and society*, pp 123–60.

Waterman, D.M., 'An early medieval horn from the River Erne', *Ulster Journal of Archaeology*, 32 (1969), pl. IV.

Whaley, Diana, 'Representations of Skalds in the sagas, 1: social and professional relations' in Poole (ed.), *Skaldsagas*, pp 285–308.

Wilson, David M., *The Bayeux Tapestry* (London, 2004).

Wilson, David M., *The Vikings in the Isle of Man* (Aarhus, 2008).

Woolf, Alex, 'Amlaíb Cuarán and the Gael, 941–81' in Seán Duffy (ed.), *Medieval Dublin*, 3 (Dublin, 2002), pp 34–43.

Woolf, Alex, *From Pictland to Alba, 789–1070* (Edinburgh, 2007).

Index